RUN WILD

RUN WILD

Boff Whalley

**SIMON &
SCHUSTER**

London · New York · Sydney · Toronto · New Delhi

A CBS COMPANY

First published in Great Britain by Simon & Schuster UK Ltd, 2012
This paperback edition published by Simon & Schuster UK Ltd, 2013

A CBS Company

Copyright © 2012 by Boff Whalley

The right of Boff Whalley to be identified as the author of this work has been
asserted by him in accordance with sections 77 and 78 of the Copyright,
Designs and Patents Act, 1988.

1 3 5 7 9 10 8 6 4 2

Simon & Schuster UK Ltd
1st Floor
222 Gray's Inn Road
London WC1X 8HB

www.simonandschuster.co.uk

Simon & Schuster Australia,
Sydney

Simon & Schuster India,
New Delhi

A CIP catalogue record for this book is available from the British Library

ISBN: 978-1-47110-180-9
Ebook ISBN: 978-1-47110-181-6

Typeset by Hewer Text UK Ltd, Edinburgh
Printed and bound in the UK by CPI Group (UK) Ltd, Croydon, CR0 4YY

To Casey, Maisy and Johnny Johnny R. Mutt

Introduction

Two personally memorable things happened in 1981 – I ran my first (and only) road marathon, and I started a band. For the following five years the band built up an audience, recorded several albums and began touring around the world. And the running? I gave it up (city-centre running failed – and still fails – to spark my imagination). Until, that is, one evening in 1986 when my dad convinced me to go and watch a local hill race taking place on the fells of northern England. I'd seen photographs, but nothing prepared me for the compelling thrill of watching 200 runners, spattered in mud, spit and sweat, tumbling down the steep, rocky descent of a small mountainside towards the finish, smiling and gasping in equal measure. The route they'd taken would have been a good half-day's walk; they'd burned up and down the fellside in less than forty-five minutes. I was hooked.

Ever since then I've balanced a life of late-night concert halls, tour buses, airports and hotel lobbies against the unquenchable urge to get out of the cities and onto the trails, heading anywhere that leads upwards and outwards. The contrast between the two sides of life couldn't be greater – but it works for me, because the extremes are complementary, each a counterpart to the other. Touring around Europe or the United States for a month in close confines with seven other people, watching Alpine or Californian mountain skylines through the windows of a bus, leaving clubs and concert halls at 3 a.m. to catch a few hours' sleep before setting off again the following morning – how could it possibly dovetail into the everyday discipline required of a dedicated trail runner? In truth, I never asked myself that question. Being in a band was my life, my work; but once I'd discovered the ensnaring power of off-road running, there was no option other than to make both work for me.

The band is called Chumbawamba and, to most people, we had just one 'hit' song, called 'Tubthumping', that was built around a chorus of: *I get knocked down, but I get up again.* Which, funnily enough, is incredibly apt as a description of trail running. Self-determination. Falling, pulling yourself up, carrying on. Optimism and confidence. Tree roots, loose rocks, mud and bloody scrapes. And always, despite every fall and trip, every lung-bursting climb that brings you to your knees, getting up again.

And in those thirty years of being in a band, I've learnt to grab running opportunities when I can. Sometimes it means missing meals or sleep (or both) but that dash towards the wildness is always worth it. City parks, riverbanks, canals, woods, fields, anything green, muddy, wet, natural and alive. Some venues make it easy. In Switzerland, Germany, Austria and Italy there are venues within easy running distance of mountain ranges. Scotland's twin cities Glasgow and Edinburgh both boast short bus rides to magnificent mountains. Eastern Europe, North America and Canada, Mediterranean Europe, Scandinavia – everywhere there are accessible, runnable trails to seek out.

On a tour of Japan in 1990, I filled a day off by running up (and down) Mount Fuji. Before a concert in Hebden Bridge, nestled below the English Pennine hills, I bailed out of the tour bus and ran the last fifteen miles to the venue over the winter fells. Playing in Lucerne, Switzerland, meant being able to run up the 6,000-feet Mount Pilatus that towers over the city – with its incredible summit views of the Eiger and the Jungfrau. The adrenalin surge of descending from a mountain in time to shower, sound-check and perform undoubtedly feeds into the rush of playing live; the running enriches the whole experience of touring, adding a dimension of adventure and exploration that can become drained by long journeys and windowless dressing rooms.

This book is, somehow, the slow-burning result of a quarter of a century of adrenalin-fuelled runs and races. It's a book born from the realization that there is a gap, at the heart of our experience as runners, between our feet and the earth. A disconnection between our natural self-propelling motion and the dirt, water, grass and rock we move over. Being in a band (an occupation drawn in straight asphalt lines between urban centres) has meant having to fight to keep that feet–earth connection – but it's a fight I still enjoy. What this book *isn't* is a how-to guide or a training plan. This book isn't like other books about running. It isn't full of motivational stories to get you lacing up your shoes and heading for the door. It doesn't contain any exercises, tactics or secrets on how to be a better runner. It's a puzzle of a book; it doesn't go

3

where you might expect it to go. This is what I believe running can be – unpredictable and surprising.

It offers encouragement but not advice; as someone who has made my living from travelling all day to play in smoke-filled concert halls, I'm decidedly unqualified to be giving runners advice. What I can offer is hope and optimism. Wild running – on trails, paths, fells and mountains – is gradually becoming more popular, not least because of our increasing understanding of the fragile ecology of the planet. We're relearning our history, rediscovering our roots. Replanting our feet in the soil.

And I can offer, too, some of the snotty belligerence that comes from being in a band like Chumbawamba – a kick aimed at the arse of the big city marathon, that Goliath of modern running. Wild running is the perfect antidote to that mammoth, and is additionally (by a twisting, higgledy-piggledy route crossing paths with back-to-nature evangelists Thoreau, Wordsworth and Muir among others) a way back to the simple love affair between our running feet and the twisting, higgledy-piggledy world we live in.

If this book goes off at tangents, gets lost, slows, quickens and loops back around to a place it left several chapters earlier – then that's because it's a book about that kind of running. Off-road, wild running; running as adventure, as play, and as a way of getting back to that simplest of relationships – the one between our feet and the earth.

People want to run. And apparently more and more of them, despite the current recession, are buying running shoes, paying inflated race fees, reading those how-to books and joining gyms, all in order to get in training to race their demons – and specifically the demon of a comfortable, twenty-first-century indolence – to prove to themselves that they're winners. And isn't that a good thing? Isn't that a change for the better in this age of the supersized beefburger, the airport travelator and the remote control? Well, yes and no. Of course it's good to see people being motivated and enthused, great to see people getting off the couch and into a pair of running shorts. But let's suppose that instead of jogging off down the street (keep turning left at every road junction and you'll eventually get back home) people headed for the grass and woods, for the trails and paths. Let's suppose that people replaced the easy, all-pervasive lure of the city marathon with the world of birdsong, cloudbursts and mud. Replaced the structure of the training plan with the freedom of following their nose. The taped, marked, marshalled roads with the adventure of *not knowing exactly where they were going to go*. That, to my mind, would be winning. No demons, just you and the world, working it out together.

We all of us run for health, fitness and wellbeing. To give our bodies a general sense of purpose – creating, in this hurly-burly world, space to think, space to breathe. But don't we also want our running to reclaim a connection with the earth beneath our running-shoe soles, a renewed awareness of the natural world and a link to our physiological history? We evolved to run. To move over our earth quickly, for long distances, in order to hunt, to eat and to communicate. It's good for our bodies, and good for our heads; historically and physiologically, it's part of what we are.

The sense of achievement which marathon runners are so eager to pursue is real, it's tangible. But running 26 miles and 385 yards along claustrophobic, smog-fast, paved city streets achieves little of that 'health, fitness and wellbeing'. It dislocates us from our natural link to both the earth and to why we run. It blinds us to the fact that just beyond the traffic-coned, orange-taped city ring roads is an enriched and enhanced version of running. Running without the glamour, the ease and the carnival; running as something personal, brave and unfamiliar.

So, in short, this is a plea. A plea to any would-be marathon runner to stop for a minute and think about what you're about to embark upon. You want a racing challenge? There are vast networks of countryside trail and pathway (with recognized and specific races and challenges for any distance from 5 kilometres to 100 miles) both inside and outside every city. Want to lose weight? Nature's rough and rolling floors will burn fat much faster than any super-smooth sidewalk, and will preserve your bones and joints better than the inelastic and unforgiving asphalt. Space and time to think, to breathe? Be alone on a hilltop, beside a river, in the dense heart of a forest. Stop and listen.

What you'll forfeit by deprogramming yourself from the cult of the marathon is simple: you'll lose the chance to tell your neighbours and friends that you 'ran a marathon'. That's all. What you'll gain is a connection to the planet that you couldn't dream of. A way of running that exercises your entire body, not just the identical stretch and pull of the same few muscles. A new look at the world, at the way seasons and years change your surroundings. A freedom from the dead weight of fixed measurements (the joy of liberation from the ubiquitous 26.2 miles!) and a gloriously gut-wrenching separation from the clock, from the tick tick tick which paces that sidewalk-jarring left, right, left, right, left, right, left . . .

In writing this book, I escaped from the band for a year to the USA and set myself the task of transferring the enthusiasm and excitement I have for wild running onto the page. I ran trails, ran races, ran back into my own history and beyond – past the words of poets and philosophers that continue to inspire and nourish my love of off-road running – and then I wrote it all down, wanting nothing more than to make that enthusiasm infectious. In short, here's me, tugging at the sleeve of your running top, saying, come and look at this, over here. Try it! Run wild!

1

It's mid-December and Britain is shivering beneath two feet of snow. It seems that the British aren't prepared for snowfall, ever – the newspapers and radio phone-in shows are piled high with worried talk of icy roads, stricken and abandoned cars, grounded aeroplanes and postponed sporting events. The Great British pluck – the Spirit of the Blitz and all that – has been cold-shouldered in favour of a nationwide, collective, worried moan. Me, I'm escaping into the heart of it, heading up to the Lake District to pull on some thermals and run up into the mountains. It's an early Christmas present; I've spent months writing and rewriting this book and I've missed the dramatic and sometimes spectacular scenery up in this north-west corner of England.

The drive to the Lake District takes me along the A65, on what I've jokingly called 'Joggers' Lane' ever since I first drove along it – its urban stretch, weaving westwards along the valley from industrial Leeds, is a favourite road for runners. On both sides of the road are fields, a river valley, woods, and miles and miles of paths, but for some reason people stick to this ten-mile urban stretch of busy road, even in the snow, choked up by the commuting cars and two-ton goods lorries thundering past – see, there they are as I drive, reflective jackets and woolly hats, up and down and up and down the fume-choked pavements. The road eventually snakes out and across the Pennine hills and into the Lake District, and by the time I'm in the wintry heart of the Lakes it's already after 4 p.m. and the winter sun is sinking lazily into the Irish Sea.

A quick change and I'm off, running straight out of the town of Ambleside and onto small lanes winding outwards and upwards, lanes becoming tracks becoming trails becoming the vaguest of paths, all under snow. The sunlight grows redder behind me and it begins to get cooler and darker. Up, up, up towards the skyline hanging like a starched apron between Dove Crag and Red Screes until, after an hour, I crest the top at its lowest point. It's getting dark now, properly dark, the cloudless sky losing the last thin thread of an orange glow, but fortunately I can see well enough to follow the route, to watch my own feet in the deepening snow, and it's easy to see the summit of Red Screes off to the east, where I'm headed. As I top one more low, false summit there's a sudden blast of light, bright and shocking. I stop. It's the moon, right in front of me, a huge glow-in-the-dark disc, big as a planet. I reach the ridge and stand with the last of the sunlight behind me and the fierce glow of the moon in front; I have two shadows.

On up to the mountain's peak, only 6 p.m. and the stars coming out. Puffing and panting through the snowdrifts and jogging, heavy footed, into the understated drama of the mountain's high point, a plateau with two small tarns hemmed in by tumbledown rocks. I stop for a few minutes, turning to follow the circumference, an unbroken circle of uneven, spectacular horizon. The snow is sparkling in tiny

9

random twinkles in the moonlight, and the lights of small Lakeland villages gather and cluster far below. It's almost Christmas, and I'm the only person in the world with this view. I haven't got a camera, but I have a memory now, a memory I can carry around forever. And this, all of it, the dark sky and white mountains, the moonlight, the sparkling, untrodden snow, and my two studded feet planted into the landscape – this is what I call running.

2

It's a golden, fresh November evening in a quiet outpost of the past on the northern tip of New York's Staten Island, grass brittle and yellowing at the end of a long, hot summer. Birds chase and call, insects buzz drunkenly on the last of the summer's pollen and squirrels race each other up and down and around the trees, scattering fallen leaves. There's a chill in the air, a gentle briskness that drifts in from the sea and up to the old Fort Wadsworth, its stone arches empty, tall and silent – a lingering dusk and the sun just a pale imitation of itself, heading down, down, down to the Atlantic's stretched ribbon of a horizon. I sit on the white stone wall overlooking this incredible view of ocean and sky and the jagged skylines of Manhattan and Brooklyn. There's an old gun, part of the fort's defences, now set in position and coated with anti-rust paint. It points directly up towards the Verrazano-Narrows Bridge, a two-tiered arc spanning the water. There's a hum of distant traffic, the chug-chug-chug of small boats, and little else.

Tomorrow morning will be different. Fort Wadsworth will wake – beating the sunrise by an hour – to a barrage of music, cars, voices, buses and megaphones, along with the sizzle, whoosh and pop of a hundred food

11

stalls; hot dogs, burgers, eggs and sausages, a light cloud of fat hanging between sky and earth, clinging to the pre-dawn trees. People in expensive running shoes will tumble out of vehicles, gradually filling the park with Lycra tops and leg-stretches, rock music and off-the-cuff motivational speeches disguised as small talk. Bloated on tonight's carbo-loading, they'll join the growing queues for the lines of green and blue plastic Portaloos, tie and re-tie their laces, rub their thighs with Vaseline and check their watches, and check their watches, and check their watches again. Outside broad-casting wagons prickly with antennae will buzz and drone as gloved and earmuffed presenters under TV lights will talk about the weather and clutch micro-phones and grip coffee cups. Eventually, approaching 9 a.m., 45,000 people will be herded and directed and hurried and harried by several hundred volunteers into vast waiting areas, their possessions – several changes of clothing, fistfuls of energy bars, asthma inhalers, post-race lotions and potions – piled into a fleet of UPS trucks that will drive off in convoy under police escort towards Central Park, Manhattan. It's the annual New York City Marathon.

3

I've been in America now for three months, waiting eagerly for this morning, for this legendary race. But I'm not among this gathering mass of leg-stretches and nipple cream to do the marathon – I'm here to watch. To try to understand why people do this. Actually, that's a lie – I've long since given up trying to understand this religious communion with the pavement, this Sunday Service at the shrine of concrete, feed-stations and chafing thighs. I've given up trying to rationalize the marathon's obsessive straight-line repetitiveness, its car-mounted digital clocks and its utter dislocation from the natural world around us. No, I'm here to watch because I have a more sinister agenda than either participating in the race or standing at the roadside shouting 'Good job!' at passing relatives: I want to breathe in the sheer madness of the marathon in order to spew it back out, half digested onto the pages of this book. To examine how we've got to this, here in New York on a Sunday in November, this carnival of barely disguised personal motivation plans and loudly branded, overpriced athletics wear. This version of running that has become, to all intents and purposes, a multi-national industry. Moreover, I'm here to put this regimented march of a race into a context; a context of the running that could, and can, happen in all those places that *aren't* the smog-bound, hemmed-in carnival of the city marathon – places within reach of almost all of us, places thick with woodland, meadow, mountain; path, track, trail; grass, mud, rock; and space, both inside and outside of us.

This book isn't a snipe at the 45,000 people running along New York's streets today, or the many thousands of spectators who'll line the route whooping and ringing their ASICS-sponsored bells and holding up placards urging on their loved ones. Neither is this a book whose sole aim is to take cheap shots at the city marathon. Rather, it's an attempt to see the marathon as cultural colossus, as corporate Leviathan obsessed above all else with size, and set it against an overlooked version of running that exists in the long, long shadow of its overbearing bigger cousin. A version of running as a relatively simple and natural sport. Inexpensive, life-affirming and unquestionably good for our heads, legs and hearts.

I'm approaching my fiftieth birthday and I feel the urge to be fit and healthy now more than ever before. I have a new baby boy and a year's sabbatical from what I loosely call my day job – writing songs, playing guitar – determined to spend my fiftieth year running through new places, new experiences. I want to discover what it is about running that has sustained me for the past twenty-five years; I want to explore the culture, history and politics of running, and by default, why I've chosen to reject the compelling lure of the city road marathon.

The marathon is currently without doubt the major attraction in running. It presents itself as the perfect modern-day challenge; combining three to five hours of running with accessibility, audience participation, TV coverage, and plenty of toilets, sponges and cups of free Gatorade. In a word (actually three words combined into a catchphrase), the marathon gives us *ease of use*. *Webster's Dictionary* says: ' "Ease of use" refers to the property of a product or thing that a user can operate without having to overcome a steep learning curve. Things with high ease of use will be intuitive to the average user in the target market for the product.'

We're surrounded by ease of use. Some of it good, some of it bad. Good in the sense that some things are (forgive me) easier to use. Bad in the sense that 'ease of use' can kill our imagination, limit our sense of wonder, stifle our creativity and fence off the unknown. This book is a plea for runners – and I include those who haven't run yet – to see that there are options outside the ubiquitous city marathon; that somewhere away from that world of ease-of-use target marketing there's a real world of discovery and adventure.

I've been running now for over a quarter of a century – longer if I include the running I did without realizing I was 'a runner' – and in that time I've gradually, step by step, managed to jettison both the desperate tyranny of the clock and the repetitive grind of the pavement. Somewhere along the way – in that chaotic storeroom of my head labelled 'things I think about while running trails' – I decided to write this book; to try to make sense of (as Primo Levi puts it) this 'labyrinthine tangle of yeses and nos'.

Having arrived on America's East Coast in a humid mid-August (over 95°F) from northern England (you'll be lucky if it reaches 65°F, mate), I head straight for the air-conditioned bookshop. Actually I hunt out the nearest woodland trail first, but this story begins in earnest at Barnes & Noble, a huge redbrick cube flanked by super-sized clothes stores by the side of a six-lane road along the Delaware–Pennsylvania border. This is mall country; four-wheel-drives park in clusters as close as possible to the main mall entrances. Nobody wants to walk (or run) far, if they can help it. Through the bookstore's doors a woman behind a counter smiles and greets me as I walk in; she's demonstrating digital book readers with scary enthusiasm. I return the smile and quickly carry on to a sports section that would cover half a baseball field. Past the shelves full of pictures of men in body armour and tights, past the gun manuals and the ghost-written autobiographies, and here we are – running. Three shelves' worth, big fat books oozing sweat and stretches, glossy well-heeled athletes on every cover, all brand-new shoes, sunny smiles and light vests. Running porn, down to the shoddy proofreading and the badly reproduced photographs of 'I-just-finished' agonized, sweating bodies. Rows and rows of spines to run your finger along . . .

Let's see.

From Around the Block to Marathon Running.
Starting Marathon Training.
How to Run Your First Marathon.
Run a Marathon in Three Months.
Essential Marathon Running.
A Marathon Runner's Handbook.
Nutrition for Marathon Running.
Idiot's Guide to Marathon Running.

Marathon Running for Mortals.
Marathon Running from Beginner to Elite.
(etc., etc., etc.)

The titles alone reek of body odour, pain and the joyless humdrum of miles and miles of accumulated city streets. I pick them out one at a time, flicking through the pages, my fascination wilting beneath an onslaught of twenty-week training programmes and motivational coaching; self-help with shorts on.

At this point – we're barely over the starting line – I need to explain something. I'm not a negative person. I'm not an example of what those bubbly, smiley self-motivators call a 'whiner'. I don't hang around marathon race start lines muttering darkly to myself, or harangue stray road runners about the demon blacktop and the evil of city smog. I'm a positive enough thinker. Often annoyingly so. I wake up every morning wondering how I got so lucky with life, with friends, family and health, and – as someone who makes a living writing and playing music – I'm still startled when I read interviews with million-selling musicians who whinge about their working lives, who don't see the irony in detailing the distress and drudgery of making another million-selling album or the angst and agony of playing in front of an adoring audience.

I'm a positive person. From my perspective, that's very different from being a *positive thinker*. For what runs through the entire gamut of those shelves and shelves of books about running – or, more accurately, books about running a marathon – is the sentimentalized, smiley-faced glow of the Positive Thinking industry with its defiantly upbeat sense of success and achievement. There's a belief in these books that the main goal of running is to achieve, to convince yourself that you're a winner, that you've set goals and reached them. Not to broaden your experience of the world, or of your place in it; not – and this is my worry – *to enjoy yourself.*

The rise and continued rise of the big city marathon, that gargantuan of the athletics world, is threatening to make running – or at least how I perceive running – into something utterly predictable. But somewhere beyond the straight-line repetition of fixed-distance tarmac racing, beyond the billboards and TV screens and websites, there's a smudge of a dirt path leading off, outwards, into a world beyond that city marathon. And that's where this book stakes its claim – on that path heading outwards, heading towards the mud, rock, forest and tree-root tangle of surprise and unpredictability.

4

The first serious race I ever ran was a marathon. Bolton, 1981, – northern England's first 'mass marathon', right at the start of the boom in road running, the grim and ordinary streets full of bunting, well-wishers and sponsored giveaways. Locally famous DJ Jimmy Savile officially started the race wearing a gold lamé tracksuit and then ran the whole 26.2 miles smoking huge cigars. I know because I ran with him for a while, until the unremitting servility of the DJ-loving spectators lining the streets (I barely noticed the cigar smoke, strangely enough) scared me into running fast enough to leave him behind. (In fairness he was probably three times my age and likely as not raising money for a local hospital.)

My friend Dan and me, we'd decided on a whim to enter the marathon. It was a novelty; a conversation point. It was the same sense of wanting to experience the peculiar that had led us to hitch to London to see Prince Charles and Lady Diana's wedding just one month earlier. We'd lately discovered hitch-hiking and for a while spent our time heading off to concerts, to cities, to events, catching up on the world as it opened up to us. Staying in people's flats, sleeping in bus shelters, in churches, anywhere we could climb into after dark. We once spent a month sleeping up on the highest tier of seating in an athletics stadium in Paris, sneaking out each morning as the first tracksuited athletes began their stretches on the track far below. We filled up with experiences, living on the little money we had and on the time borrowed from lack of responsibilities – as long as we could eat, we were happy, buzzing around with our sleeping bags and bad haircuts. So when we heard about this 'marathon' (in inverted commas, of course) we entered it straight away – more in a spirit of adventure than anything else.

The royal wedding and the Bolton Marathon had their similarities – huge crowds of well-wishers, a long hot day spent on inhospitable city streets and at least two of the participants (me and Diana) later left wondering whether this was really such a good idea in the first place. On marathon day, Bolton, all stone civic buildings and concrete supermarkets, burst into life. Shopkeepers gave away free ice lollies en route, groups of men sat outside pubs drinking pints of beer and shouting that we 'must be daft!' and runners vomited openly as they ran. I got round in a few minutes over four hours. I'd done very little training and wore a pair of worn Hi-Tec Silver Shadow running shoes, boasting a collapsing mid-sole and a raised heel-counter, bought for less than £20 and in use far beyond their natural lifespan. Dan finished not far behind me and we put the whole affair down to 'experience'. Neither of us would ever run a city marathon again.

It isn't that I didn't enjoy the race – I did, in a peculiar and cursory way – but I wasn't left with any sense of what running was, and is, and could be. Before this I'd run at school, but again without any sense of why I was doing it.

Earlier, in the fading Polaroid blur of the mid-1970s, with the northern English rain falling like a bad mood onto our skinny white schoolboy frames, we'd huddle against the school changing-room doors as teachers ticked boxes and smoked cigs before waving us off on our weekly Wednesday cross-country run. We jogged dutifully out of the front gate, round the local housing estate and down the track to the old stone canal bridge, where we stopped abruptly; too far for teachers to bother finding us, we threw stones into the water for twenty minutes before jogging back feigning tiredness. It was a game we played, a game based on the understanding that, somehow, running was more a punishment than a games lesson; it's what you had to do when the teacher wanted to put his feet up and read the local paper or catch up on some marking. It was uninspired and uninspiring; the ultimate misnomer of physical education – not particularly physical and of no educational value. Off you go, lads, don't forget your cigarettes.

Running the Bolton Marathon confirmed my lack of interest in the Olympian ideal of those hallowed 26 miles and 385 yards. I wanted the spectacle, the experience; for those four or five hours. But I didn't want it for life. What I wanted for life – and, I think, what I still want – is for it all to be one big, marvellous adventure. A sweat-soaked, exhausting, exciting, helped-along-the-way adventure. And if my running could somehow be like that, too, then all the better.

5

The sun crept up behind me, nipped first at my ankles and calves, and then flooded across the incredible mountain-top landscape of the Langdale Pikes. I was halfway between Harrison Stickle and Pike o'Stickle, 2,000 feet up among the rocks and crags of the English Lake District. In spite of a steady intake of bananas and chocolate, my blood sugar level was so low I felt emptied out, vacant and weak. Still, I could fix my eyes on the horizon and manage a smile; my fingers were wrapped around an Ordnance Survey map sprinkled with pikes, gables, knotts, dodds, fells and sandals and I was roughly halfway (with more than ten hours completed) round a twenty-four-hour mountain challenge that boasts the following statistics: 42 mountain peaks, 70 miles of running and 28,000 feet of climbing, all in under twenty-four hours.

Despite the number-crunching, the route planning and all the logistical paraphernalia of attempting what's known as 'the Bob Graham Round' (named after its legendary initiator), at that point it was impossible – in the here and now of a spectacular breaking dawn and a high-level pano-rama of summits and ridges – to forget what a stunningly perfect day this was, a day (and a night) trotting around the roof of England. The Round was first completed in

1932 by Bob Graham, wearing a pyjama top, baggy shorts and tennis plimsolls and fortifying himself with bread, butter and boiled eggs. A keen fell walker and runner, he traced a route across those forty-two peaks and set a record that held for almost thirty years; and in so doing he plotted the definitive Lakeland challenge. In visiting all the major peaks in the area, the Round draws a high-level circle around all of England's highest mountains – a one-lap loop balanced at the point where the land rises to meet the sky.

For my attempt on the Bob Graham Round I was joined along the way by supporters and route finders, runners willing to spend several hours each carrying water, sandwiches and sugary sweets up and down the harshest corner of England. The sun was climbing now and our shadows were shortening. Every so often I looked across to the mountains stretched like huge grey curtains around me, mountains I'd run over earlier in the day, climbs that seemed so long ago, so far away. Exhausting as all this was, the sense of relief began to grow; and gradually the scope of the challenge gave way to the idea that all of this was really just an excuse for what my grandad would call 'a right good day out'.

Two weeks earlier, setting off after dark from the traditional starting point in Keswick, I'd ploughed up the first 3,000-foot climb and into low cloud so dense it completely blanketed me from the outside world and from all the sense and reason I take for granted; even the clearest of paths to the summit was difficult to follow and the light from my headlamp bounced back at me from a million specks of thick, wet mist. The stuff clung to me and didn't let go. The rain switched from drizzle to stair rods as I careered off Skiddaw's summit following a compass bearing, disorientated and hesitant. I crossed swollen becks and trogged through moss-soaked wasteland, unable to see any shape or feature worth the Ordnance Survey's bother. I finally reached the first checkpoint – a road crossing in the tiny grey-slate hamlet of Threlkeld – around five hours later, an hour and forty minutes behind schedule. The rain intensified; the lowlands were turning into treacly quagmires, rivers into torrents. Knowing I would never have made it round in under twenty-four hours I had to abandon the attempt, stripped off my drenched clothing and decided to have another go two weeks later.

The second time, stomping uneasily down to Honister with around four hours more running to go, muscles cramping and sweat pouring out of me as fast as I could force water down my throat, I realized that the deed was as good as done: in a few more hours I'd be shuffling up the main street in Keswick. My time, aside from finishing under twenty-four hours, was of no interest to me. I'd decided a year ago to do the Bob Graham Round not only because of the challenge and the achievement but for its history and its tradition; and for a chance to experience something utterly memorable and notoriously wild. A connection down through the years, a string of mountain tops which haven't changed since the first attempts at this Round, and a sport with its feet rooted in a deeply felt sense of being able to mesh with the natural world towering above us. And who can resist a challenge set by a man wearing a pyjama top?

Pyjamas aside, it would be naïve of me to describe the

Bob Graham Round as just 'a right good day out'. The surviving photograph of Bob himself on the Round, broad grin and baggy socks, belies (as do any photographs of myself during the same challenge, thumbs up and smiling) both the sheer effort of will on the day and the many years of training and mountain craft which go into attempting something like this. (Anyone in any doubt should read Richard Askwith's account of the pain and effort of years of attempts on the Bob Graham Round in his book *Feet in the Clouds*). As well as the chance to experience a day-and-night panorama of dawn-pink peaks and dusk-grey valleys, it tests the fabric of your body, stretching and pulling at every muscle, bone and blister, while at the same time bombarding your imagination with the temptation of stopping, giving up, pulling out, sitting down and going to sleep.

During the night-time hours, mountains appeared as if from nowhere, looming and taunting. Bogs clutched, puddles sucked, heather grabbed and stones bit and snapped. My feet wouldn't work properly. My maps were redrawn as meaningless squiggles and symbols. My food supplies consisted of everything I couldn't stomach. But then . . . drinking ice-cold water from a stream below the vast natural pyramid of Great Gable, I found my feet again, tripping easily across loose rock 3,000 feet high and feeling closer to sky than to sea. And then this body wasn't stretching and pulling any more, it was singing its place on the earth. Look at me, Ma! Top of the world!

At the end of the Round, as the reddest of red suns slid away to my left, a million stars came out with a vengeance, pinpointing the last few miles to the Moot Hall just three minutes over twenty-three hours. The achievement wasn't in the finishing but in the doing, the intense thrill of a long, long day's reacquaintance with (as Eric Dezenhall puts it), 'life's friction'. That's what I strive for, that's what running means to me – the utterly human quest for the wild, natural, joyful rub of life's friction.

6

Early October and up in New York the sun's still out with a vengeance. It's 9 a.m. in Wolfe's Pond Park, Staten Island, seven miles down Hylan Boulevard from Fort Wadsworth and the Verrazano-Narrows Bridge into Brooklyn, the official start of the New York City Marathon. It's just a month before Staten Island will swarm with upwards of 45,000 nervous and expectant runners and I'm here to do a trail race around the woods and beaches of Wolfe's Pond, almost 200 acres of woodland surrounding a former tidal inlet, now a freshwater lake. New York City once contained 224,000 acres of freshwater wetland. The wetland ecosystem can slow erosion, prevent flooding, filter pollutants and slow global warming by converting carbon dioxide into oxygen. Nevertheless, over the past 200 years most of this land has been destroyed and given over to more buildings and roads, until now only 2,000 acres of freshwater wetland remain in the city – and along with the loss of a valued ecosystem, many species that once called the wetland home have been lost forever. Almost lost now, marooned in the city's concrete ocean, the remaining natural spaces like Wolfe's Pond Park are places to treasure. Places to play, to run, to escape.

I'm here to try to understand why those tens of

thousands of runners will congregate a few miles up the road (always the road) and pay between $200 and $300 to run along the Five Boroughs' asphalt when there are places like Wolfe's Pond offering something more fundamentally, powerfully seductive and captivating. You want carnival atmosphere, too? The race organizer today has thoughtfully brought along not only his own public address system to belt out a variety of fist-pumping, motivational rock classics, he's also hired a small band to play live Beatles cover versions. There's the static, boom and crackle of connecting wires before the band lurch into 'I've Got a Feeling'. You want razzamatazz? Three American flags flutter beside a gazebo, and a few minutes before the race we're instructed to 'doff our headwear' and stand proudly through a hideous R&B version of 'The Star-Spangled Banner'. Some put their hands to their hearts and everyone faces the flags, perhaps thinking hard about the song's composer, Francis Scott Key, a lifelong slave owner. Behind me are trestle tables piled with snacks, bagels, spreads, fruit and drinks; after the race there'll be a picnic and get-together and perhaps some dancing to the Beatles covers. The course is stringently marked, the organizer has an electric megaphone and there are volunteers, sponsors, free shirts in with the entry fee and supporters dawdling in the sun waiting for the start; and, to top it all off, the accurately measured race route has four drinks' stations, digital timing and computerized results.

Thus being stuffed with carnival-style peripherals I'd expected a few more runners than the forty or so who turn up on a gloriously sunny autumn morning, those seven easy miles down Hylan Boulevard from next month's New

York City Marathon start. Forty! Three flags and a live band for forty runners. I'm tempted to claim that this race provides everything the marathon runner could want – apart from distance (today's race is six miles), the lure of the throng and the attendant carnival. In reality, I know what's really missing here: the culture of recognition, of the safe-in-what-you-know rules of engagement, of pre-arrangement, plan, security and caution. Trails go up and down, they twist and they turn. No amount of public address, megaphone and R&B warbling can disguise the sheer unpredictability of *leaving the road*. It's dark in there. What happened to the crowds? To the music? To the big clock with the green flashing LED numerals? What happened to the straight, straight road ahead?

We love what we know. The marathon is what we all know. Any runner will testify to the fact that the question most asked of runners by non-runners is '*Have you ever done a marathon?*' Why? Because everyone knows it. Because the bookshelves in the bookstores are buckling under the weight of books about running the marathon. It's an institution, a benchmark: but a lazy, overplayed and tame one. That's not the fault of the people who run them, it's the end result of overweight, size-obsessed organizations, bloated with sponsorship and media coverage. When people ask me if I've ever run a marathon, I want to tell them about races that reduce the city marathon to little more than an ease-of-use experience – races without traffic cones and straight lines. Races that shock and surprise. That don't go where you think they might go. The descent you didn't expect, loose soil falling away, having to grasp at tree trunks. The storm cloud suddenly bursting with a ferocity your clothing can't understand. The mountain path narrowing to a ridge, no wider than your two feet, the ground on both sides of you disappearing into cloud, the sudden fear that forces you to stoop and clutch the rock as you move. The snow drifting deeper, deeper, coyly inviting, hiding peat bogs and stream gullies and twist-your-ankle ditches. The moorland, barren and bleak, throwing up treasure – the remains of a crashed aeroplane, scattered and half buried, a wing here, a fuselage there. Five white hares put to flight by your stumble, unidentifiable animals everywhere, in the air (being dive-bombed high on England's Howgills mountains by a bird of prey), deep in the forest, leaping from rivers as you cross.

Wolfe's Pond Park is a wonderful place to run in, and to race in, with its jumbled mix of sandy beach, open parkland, deep, thick tree cover and the so-densely-wooded-it's-a-secret freshwater pond. It's a wonderful place to have an adventure, to scramble down muddy banks and follow small rivers, or to burst your lungs racing through, around and deep into the heart of it. And the charm of it – and the pleasure of every part of the earth not imposed upon by hewn stone and bedded concrete – is that it's a changing place, a shifting, evolving landscape. In one month this island will teem with the buzz of the big race; today forty of us tuck into the bagels, exhausted and satisfied, having saturated ourselves with a corner of the world we've never seen before.

7

One month later, a freezing New York morning, seven o'clock. Two hours to start time and the runners are swarming, moving in packs, queuing, huddling, nervously sitting down and standing up and always stretching, stretching, stretching. I read the T-shirts:

THE WORK DOESN'T START UNTIL THE PAIN KICKS IN
CHAMPIONS TRAIN, LOSERS COMPLAIN
TRAMPLE THE WEAK – HURDLE THE DEAD
NO-ONE EVER DROWNED IN SWEAT
PAIN IS JUST WEAKNESS LEAVING YOUR BODY
LOSERS QUIT WHEN THEY'RE TIRED – WINNERS NEVER
   QUIT

The 45,000 runners are to set off in 'waves', strictly shepherded batches according to estimated running speed. Everyone seems to be caught in the dilemma of how much clothing to wear, with the dawn's bitter wind wriggling through the slow-moving sea of breathable fabric. Some runners will have almost as long waiting to cross the starting line as it takes others to run the course – the nervous energy is palpable. The Verrazano Bridge, arched and arcing away from Fort Wadsworth

31

before plunging into the southernmost tip of Brooklyn, has been closed to traffic and waits like a sentry for the crack of the gun, the padding thrum of thousands of pairs of feet, and the thick, panting invasion of half a town's worth of runners.

It's exciting, there's no denying it. The air crackles with expectation, the news crews repeat themselves, and the doors on the long, long lines of plastic toilets go bang bang bang, arrhythmic and irritating. Gloves on, gloves off? Hat, headband, long sleeves or short? Tights, knee-lengths, hooded top? It's a chill wind blowing in off the bay, and you can never trust the weather forecast, not on a day like today, not on a day when the wrong choice of shirt can cost you precious minutes. In among the runners, occasionally guided towards the news team camera's lights, are celebrity chefs, ex-footballers, TV presenters and (today's hero) a Chilean miner, Edison Peña, who until only a few weeks ago had been trapped half a mile underground in a collapsed mine for sixty-nine days. Now, understandably, he looks like he wants space to warm up and stretch, but he's kept busy with interviews and well-wishers. One knee is already strapped and bandaged – and, looking round, I can't help but notice all the straps and dressings, compression hose and muscle tape holding all those legs together, patching up ankles, cushioning knees as they wait, cold, in the queue for the toilets.

8

Long before I'd ever heard of the marathon I was drawn to running by comic-book hero Alf Tupper from the *Rover* who, fuelled on fish and chips and racing in tatty vest and shoes, hitch-hiked to races and customarily beat all the athletic toffs with their clean white vests and plummy accents. Alf ran cross-country, and was invariably either pushed in a river, overtaken by cheats taking short cuts, or got lost in snow blizzards.

> *The wind howled and a line of spruce trees bent over in the gusts. It was impossible to see for more than a few yards. 'Lummy,' muttered Alf grimly, 'this is a nice afternoon out!' He reached a ditch and only after a search found the plank that spanned the icy water. Through the driving snow he located a Dutch barn that showed him he was still on his course. Alf shivered and ran past the barn.*
>
> *He was plastered with snow. It lay thick in his shaggy hair. Through another drift he emerged from the lane. Now he was facing north-east and full into the wind. He had to keep his head right down to breathe. An oak tree gave him his bearings and then, out of the blizzard, came the shape of Bridgely School from which the race had started and which was also the finishing point.*

*Alf plodded slowly towards the building. He peered round
and scowled angrily. 'Why aren't the blooming judges on the
job?' he growled, for nobody was to be seen. Alf turned in
through the school gateway. Lights were shining from the
windows, for the building was being used as a dressing
room. There were shouts of 'Shut that door!' as he pushed it
open and stood on the threshold. His blurred eyes picked out
Harden-Hughes, the famous cross-country runner.*

*'So you beat me to it, Noel!' he exclaimed. Harden-
Hughes stared at him in amazement. 'You haven't finished
the course?' he gasped. Alf stared at him in surprise. 'What
d'you suppose I've been doing – looking for birds' nests?' he
scoffed. Stewart Farr, the secretary of the Three Counties
Association, came forward. 'The race was abandoned,' he
said. 'It wasn't fit for a dog to be out – and we abandoned
it after the second lap.'*

*'I was out in it,' snapped Alf. He gave a sniff as he looked
down the room at the other competitors, most of whom had
finished changing. 'Lot of cissies!'*

That's how I imagined running – navigating through blizzards and beating the toffs. Simple! But before I ever ran,
I looked at maps. The Ordnance Survey – Britain's national
mapping agency – charted my life. By the time I reached
my teens I was fascinated by the incredible feat of design
that could reduce a mountain range to both a readable
cipher and a work of art; despite failing Geography O
level at school I quietly stole the school's curriculum book
on map-reading. I have it still, somewhere, with my name
inked inside its cover in bubble writing. Learning about
the topography and geology of the land didn't capture my

interest; what fascinated me was how something that complex and beautiful – the abstract expressionist canvas of contours, cols, knolls and bluffs – could be used to find your way around the world. I used to wonder who designed and drew these magical coded plans, imagining Brylcreemed fellows in tweed suits and stout walking boots out in the field, armed only with sets of coloured pencils and theodolites. Picture two chaps standing around a small bog up in the Yorkshire Dales, wind whipping their knitted ties over their shoulders.

'Grid Ref 226897NE. Three feet seven inches by five feet exactly. Small bog, Ralph.'

'You sure it's a bog, Roger?'

'Of course. Inasmuch as it's boggy, yes.'

'But it's been raining as if the very devil himself had been wringing out the world's socks. I suggest this is a small depression, temporarily holding moisture.'

'I beg to differ, Ralph. Even an erosion gully would have had sufficient drainage to allow the water to run off. This brown, wet stuff has been sitting here for eons. It's a bog, I tell you.'

'Not even . . . a re-entrant?'

'A bog.'

'[Sighs] Pass me the blue pencil, Rodge.'

As I grew older I zoomed in, transferring from the imperial 1-in. to 1-mile standard hiker's map to the 1:50,000 (1 cm = 500 m) metric map, and from there to the Landranger 1:25,000. Of course, once you start getting closer and closer to every feature on the ground you can't stop – it's an addiction, and the dose must keep increasing to get the same high. The non-Ordnance Survey orienteering competition maps now get as close as 1:10,000, and include incredibly accurate renderings of cow droppings, discarded Coke cans and even your own studded footprints in the mud as you run.

Jay Griffiths is a writer with a gung-ho sense of purpose and passion. Her book *Wild* recounts a journey across the world in search of the true wildernesses. Through forest, ice and sea she braves injury, disease, danger (in bucketfuls) and, frankly, desperation in order to fully explore the idea of wildness. She's awe-inspiring and a fantastic writer, too. So much so that after surfacing from *Wild* (which I read during the year-long journey of this book) I couldn't help feeling timid and overcautious, running my finger along a map regulated by grids, forewarned and forearmed by a flattened plan of the earth. And that's silly, of course – every explorer needs a map. Maps won't, and don't, sit quietly on your bookshelves like novels, dictionaries and poetry collections – they yell at us to Get Out! Maps tug at your sleeve, cajole, plead, and make outrageous promises. All that moving, wriggling, barbed-and-fighting life, look, it's all there for you . . . and there you are, barely bigger than an atom, down below your own giant finger, scaling the brown contour lines, crossing smooth inky-blue streams and jumping across the paper-fold chasms. Jay Griffiths, of course, uses maps; we all do. I have a fleeting image of the world's great explorers deep underground on the platform of Oxford Street tube station trying to work out how to get to Cockfosters. Or Shackleton, Cook and the rest striding manfully from their B&B in Keswick and getting lost in the various ginnels and alleyways between WHSmith and the bakery on the corner.

I was eleven years old, not long out of short trousers, knocking at the plywood-panelled door of a small terraced council house off Rossendale Road in Burnley. The house sat in the middle of a group of terraces originally built for the families of men who worked in one of the local coal pits, but since the mine had long since closed the houses had become neglected, isolated and rundown. There was a scratty playground, wrecked, paint-peeled, its swings and slide broken and defaced. Seven a.m. and no one was answering my knocks. It was Col Mowbray's house – I hadn't been before, but I had it written on a scrap of paper in my pocket, number 12. In my duffel bag I had a plastic bottle of blackcurrant juice, two Penguin chocolate biscuits, a wedge of tinfoil-wrapped egg sandwiches, a V-necked woollen jumper and (the holy grail) a road map of Lancashire. There was also my mum's Pacamac in there ('in case it rains') but I kept quiet about that. Another knock, harder this time. I lived at the top of Rossendale Road and so I'd set off first, planning to collect Col on the way before meeting the rest at Willie Holt's Billiard Manufacturers in Rosegrove. Col and me and three more boys were spending our Saturday walking up Pendle Hill, three miles north of Burnley and, being only 200 feet short of proper mountain status, the local focal point.

Pendle Hill was also the infamous haunt of the Lancashire witches; we'd grown up with these stories of seventeenth-century Mother Demdyke and old Alice Nutter with her scary shape-changing cat. It wasn't until long after I'd left Burnley that I read of the actual circumstances surrounding the so-called Pendle Witches' trials and executions – how they were victims of power-seeking landowners and Church-bred suspicion and misogyny, and how ten women were hanged.

The door opened. It was Col, wearing pyjama bottoms and rubbing his eyes against the daylight.

'What time is it?'

'It's ten past seven! How come you're not ready? They'll all be waiting for us at Willie Holt's!'

He looked around, worried, and put a finger to his lips.

'Shhh. Mi' dad's asleep. Come in and wait here. I'll not be a minute.'

He stumbled off hurriedly and I crept into the room. The curtains – thick and heavy, real rugs of material – only allowed the slimmest slits of sunlight into the room, the daylight speckled with dust. Gradually, as I became accustomed to the gloom, I could see an overweight, unshaven bloke on the settee, laid out and fast asleep, knees tucked in so he could fit between the armrests. That must be Col's dad. Below the rim of the settee, in an evenly spaced row along the floor, were eight or nine empty beer bottles. I looked around the room. I'd never seen a room so untidy, so full of stuff. Stuff all over the floor, on the shelves, on the TV top, and scattered on all the furniture. Discarded stuff, thrown-away stuff, packets and paper and jars and food, toys and plates and photographs and . . . stuff. Everywhere. And with all that stuff, and Col's dad, I didn't dare move, so I stuck close to the front door and held my breath. Cos it stunk, too. It smelled of beer and animals. It was like something from a Charles Dickens book, that's what I was thinking. Reminiscent of a thieves' den, somewhere in the East

End of London. I stood there wishing Col would hurry up because I was scared stiff there, and I didn't really know why but it was something to do with feeling disorientated and puzzled and above all sad for Col, with his dead drunk dad on the sofa and his mate coming round and waking him up and him in his pyjama bottoms and all that, and not even having time to tidy up a bit. But when Col came back in the room, stuffing a packet of biscuits into his trouser pocket and clutching a bottle of Lucozade, he didn't look sad at all, he just beckoned for us to leave, slamming the door shut behind him and talking normal boy talk as if him living in a nineteenth-century Dickensian thieves' den wasn't at all unusual.

Twenty past seven and we weren't at Holt's yet. This delay was very un-maplike, of course – maps don't digress, don't shoot off somewhere unexpected. They stick to what they do best, permanently and in an orderly fashion. Most unlike life, in fact. When we finally all met up, me still thinking about how Col's dad had his beer bottles all lined up, I took out the map. The map changed the walk into an expedition; gave us the feeling of being on an adventure. We gathered round it, stabbing our fingers at the lines. It was all there, on that folded paper. We weren't catching a bus, or following an adult, or having to learn it from a teacher. It was just us and our pointing fingers and this map, off up Pendle Hill with our duffel bags and sandwiches (and Col with his biscuits). What the map did, too, was confirm that we were leaving the town. As we walked through Padiham on the outskirts of Burnley, dawdling at Gawthorpe (where the Burnley football team trained), on past the White Horse pub and up the hill to cross the main A6068 bypass, the walk became a saga, a story to tell. The map told us so; see the light grey areas, built up and populated, terraced housing, shops, schools, churches – see where that light grey ends and becomes a mottled patchwork of white and green? That's where we were. Out of the town. Away from what we knew. And as we walked further out, onto country roads and beside farmed fields and country pubs (we laughed ourselves daft at the sign reading 'Red Rock Inn Car Park'. Red rock in car park!) we somehow grew tougher and more fearless, promising ourselves that we wouldn't stop for lunch until we'd reached the hill's summit. And it was a proper haul getting there, through Sabden village's quiet Saturday calm, over the little bridge, up the road to the Nick o'Pendle and on, on past the Second World War concrete pillbox and finally across the ridge of the hill itself. Pendle summit, ten miles from my house, a whitewashed stone triangulation marker on an open moor, high above the towns and villages it overlooked. We sat with our backs to the stone post, eating sandwiches and taking it in turns to run our eggy fingers along the route we'd taken on that road map, those grubby pointed digits escaping from the grey and onto the hills.

None of us had ever walked this far. We'd heard stories of boys from Burnley who'd done it, but we didn't know anyone personally, which gave us the right to feel we were making an adventure all of our own and not one we'd learnt from a book. Twenty miles I walked that day, there and back, clutching the map. Suddenly the map meant something more than a way to get somewhere; it had become a way of getting out. It made Pendle Hill more than just a skyline we saw every day and into something tangible, sitting there on our arses in a circle around the summit, telling jokes. Most of all, as I thought about it over the coming days, the map said something about Col and his dad and their dark house, about slipping away and effecting an escape. Years later, long after I'd moved away from Burnley, I heard that Col Mowbray had died sniffing glue at a party up on the Stoops Estate, no more than a mile from where I'd called for him that morning. He'd fallen asleep on a settee, turned blue and his heart had stopped beating before anyone had realized what was happening.

A map is an open invitation to any of us to get off the roads without fearing that we may disappear into that anonymous countryside that stretches on forever, all its signposts turned around and its farmers lying in wait brandishing double-barrelled shotguns. A map can be both a prod between the ribs (go on, get your shoes on and take a run down that trail) and insurance that you'll be able to return. There are pathways back to safety! When I'm halfway up Pen-Y-Ghent in the Yorkshire Dales and see a small gaggle of school kids lolloping towards me, red-faced and giggling, I'm filled with optimism about the world. Maps give them a licence to be out here, away from the shopping malls and multiplex cinemas, away from their Wiis and Xboxes and PlayStations. The irony of the Wii-Jog (where you can go jogging from the comfort of an electronically activated floor pad in front of the TV in your living room) appals and amuses me in equal measure; but I see enough giggling groups of school kids heading up well-worn mountain tracks to stop me, I hope, turning into a caricature 'kids today don't know they're born' grumpy old man.

Burnley is a town nestled in the base of a wild green bowl, the remnants of its industry ringed by hills. Almost any way you approach Burnley means to overlook it first, and, strangely, one of the best things about the town is how easy it is to get out of it. After that first foray up Pendle Hill it became a habit to gather up friends, pack egg butties and walk upwards out of town. The Lancashire hills are traditionally described as bleak and windswept, which isn't my experience of them at all. To me and my friends they were vast, mucky-green playgrounds, places to mess around in – they weren't beautiful or scenic to us, they were just open, full of possibilities and seemingly limitless. And more – they were a world away from the redbrick drudgery of school and the scuffed concrete of the town's shopping centre. We had little respect for the countryside – nobody had ever taught us that this was a place worth respecting – and we frequently started fires and stole birds' eggs. At least it was better than pushing lit fireworks through people's letterboxes and breaking into school (the less said about that the better).

The hills were an escape, whether I knew it or not. They represented the sense of unplanned openness and freedom that terraced housing and suburbia were designed to shut off, to deny. When I read many years later about industrialization and the creation of the working factory and mill towns – with its mass migration from the villages – it became clearer that this forced movement into heavily paved, overpolluted and architecturally regimented living spaces was something that people would eventually (and naturally) try to escape from. Before the Industrial Revolution there was something of an organic connection between town and country; after it, the two became estranged, distant. Before, the natural world was in the everyday. After it, reconnecting with wildness would take time and effort. What my boyhood escapades into the countryside taught me back then wasn't about the spectacular complexity and fragility of nature, nor of its beauty, but of a lost sense of wildness and freedom. Up high on the moors to the south of Burnley is the television mast at Hameldon Hill. It was to here that me and three or four friends came after our last day of school, slogging up through the fields before climbing past the barbed wire and metal grilling surrounding the tower. Scaling it, as we'd done many times before, we could feel it swaying in the wind, clasping the iron ladders and trying to wipe the wind-forced tears from our eyes. We bound our school ties to the tower's pinnacle and descended, seeing them crack and slap high above the ground. It marked an ending, but somehow it confirmed that the future might be a bigger, more exciting, windblown affair than the relatively strict past. The sense of danger provoked as much challenge as caution. On our expeditions out to the hills, reservoirs and woods outside the town we were invariably underdressed, overconfident and aimless.

I've since learnt that a map is as much a warning as a guide, of course. Not too long ago I was running on the path leading off the summit of Pike o'Blisco in the Lake District, having slogged, wrapped up and balaclava'd, around the wintery Langdale Pikes. At 2,300 feet, Blisco is often in cloud; that day the cloud hung heavily

43

down below its shoulders, and finding a route off the mountain was a matter of either specific local knowledge (which I didn't have) or following a map and compass (which I did). I was dropping below the mist and following the stony path downwards towards the head of the valley when I saw three figures climbing up the trail towards me. As I got closer I saw it was a man with two young boys; they had on light jackets and ordinary shoes and carried no sacks (day-, ruck-, knap- or otherwise). The man stretched out a hand to get my attention, and I came to a stop. He asked, in faltering English but with a distinctly French accent, if this was the way to Scafell Pike. He pointed up the path, into the thick cloud.

'Well . . . yes, sort of. But you're a long way from Scafell Pike. And it's really cold up there, with hardly any visibility.'

I looked at the two young boys, probably aged around ten and twelve. They looked away. The man nodded.

'Ah, OK, that is good. This way then?'

Maybe he hadn't understood me.

'It's this way, but it's a long way. A very long way. Do you have a map?'

'No, but if this way then OK.'

I unzipped my bumbag and pulled out a map. Swept my fingers across its contours, arched my eyebrows and tried to enunciate very clearly. I was at my patronizing worst, and I felt like an English football fan ordering a beer in a Marseille bistro.

'We are here. See, and over here is Scafell Pike. That's a long way. The paths are very steep and dangerous. This bit here [I draw my hand across the centre of the map] is all mountains. Big mountains. Very cold. Many hours away. No roads. Scafell Pike is steep. Big. Danger.'

I could see I wasn't convincing him.

'You go down here [I pointed down the path] to the pub. Dungeon Ghyll, pub. Tavern. Bar. Nice fire. Hot chocolate. Warm.'

'OK, then is good. Thank you. Thank you.'

He gathered his two lads and carried on up the path, smiling.

As I write this, an American autumn hurricane heading our way and leaves swirling in the hairdryer heat outside, I try to stop myself smirking (only smug gits smirk!) at the news report I'd heard earlier in the week: two world-class Kenyan runners in last weekend's Quad Cities Marathon in Iowa got lost on the course. John Maina and Mark Chepses became confused when a motorbike they were following left the course (as it was supposed to do), leaving them to follow only a road lined on both sides with orange cones. They became confused and decided to head off in the direction of the motorcycle, only returning when it was clear they weren't on a twenty-five-foot strip of blacktop but in a park. They asked people for directions and rejoined the race where they'd left it. While the runners claimed unfamiliarity with the route, the race organizers stressed that both runners had neglected to attend the elite runners' meeting the previous night that walks the top competitors through the course. What happened to the practice of painting a coloured line along the roadway the entire 26.2 miles? In the Tour de France the mountain stage roads are decorated with the brush-painted names of cycling heroes, daubed in the weeks leading up to the Tour, along with exhortations to *Allez! Allez!* and Up, up, up!, while the marathon makes do with an unbroken cord of durable but slow-setting epoxy mixture in a red, or a blue, or a green – not, obviously, yellow or white, since runners may confuse the line with existing traffic markings. (It isn't supposed to be orienteering, after all.) I wonder what Alf Tupper would have made of the story, or, indeed, of the city marathons. Probably just mutter, 'Lummy!' and head off to find the nearest fish 'n' chip shop.

9

A short digression on the subject of the legendary Phyllis Pearsall, a woman hopelessly lost on her way to a party in London's posh Belgravia one night in 1935. Picture her confusion as she wandered London's labyrinthine (a Belgravia word for 'higgledy-piggledy') avenues, terraces and plain old streets looking for that house with the upstairs lights on and the trad jazz blaring. Phyllis was an artist and instead of waiting around for marathon organizers to turn up with the epoxy paint she decided to create a street map of London that would be available in book form. And she would call it the *A to Z Pocket Map* and it would change the way many of us see our capital city forever. Initial drawings and surveys for the book, which she completed with the help of only one other person, took just one year – she worked up to eighteen hours a day mapping the city's 23,000 streets. Setting up her own publishing company, she printed the first *A to Z* herself and saw it become an immediate success. The company's motto? 'On we go'. (Not that far removed from *Allez! Allez!*) Phyllis, in a typical act of selflessness and goodwill, turned the suddenly wealthy company, the Geographers' A–Z Map Co., into a trust to ensure that it was never bought out. This secured the future of her company and its employees. So far, so splendid.

During the mid-nineties I lived in London, somewhere in the middle of page forty-five, near the top of the page, actually in square 1G, just to the east of Archway Road, below the church on the corner. Goodness but this map was ugly. With its thick black mesh of criss-cross confusion, its flatness, its refusal to allow any sense of up-and-downness, topography or elevation, its lack of footpaths, waterways and trees – just a thudding, super-dense barrage of street names at odd angles. Which is the point, of course. I was in a city and I shouldn't have expected to find a stream or a footpath or, (sadly) a tree. And, yes, the *A to Z* got me from the Archway across Waterlow Park and on past Highgate Cemetery and finally, phew, to Hampstead Heath with its ponds and bird sanctuaries. But I hated it, that terrible bible of a book with its obsession with flat lines and flat typefaces, everything undecorated, frill-free. When I ran across Waterlow Park towards Hampstead Heath I wanted to see, on the map, the little boat and bathhouses, the sudden lines of thickly wooded paths. I wanted to see Highgate Cemetery for what it is – with its steeply rising spaghetti bowl of paths around those three small ponds.

And if I'm being picky, yes, I wanted a map that used the Gill Sans typeface, with its round 'o' and its double-storey lower-case 'g' (its designer Eric Gill is quoted as saying, 'A pair of spectacles is rather like a g; I will make a g rather like a pair of spectacles') all conjuring up an unashamedly old-fashioned *Englishness*. Ironically, Phyllis Pearsall was herself a typographer, and she had the typeface for the *A to Z* specially designed by (who else?) Eric Gill! Forced to rethink my yearning for some antiquated, fossilized version of 'Englishness' (and without drawing on George Orwell's 'cricket on the village green' whimsy) I suppose what I wished for was an Englishness before the flat, regulated template of internationalist city planning. By which I mean (picture me sucking a boiled sweet and harrumphing at the beastliness of it all) the everything-square grids-and-capitals of modern urban America.

One thing America does well (and there are some things it does so much better than the British. But that's another book) is the weather. I love running in my homeland northern English weather, the hazy greys and seemingly perpetual damp. Squishy moorland, heather heavy with dew (in the morning), rain (in the afternoon) and mist (in the evening, when the ghost of Heathcliff roams the land). Sun and snow as novelties, to be enjoyed to the full because they won't stay long. Mountaintop gales, one minute ready to throw you onto the crags below and, the next, cooling and calming and drying out your sodden shorts and squelchy fell-running shoes. But America – a land of extremes in so many ways – has all this but magnified and exaggerated. I used to watch Hollywood films and scoff at the fake rainstorms. Gene Kelly, singin' in the rain on some stiflingly dry set off Sunset Boulevard, with stage-hands throwing buckets of water from above. That's not rain! I used to think. Rain just doesn't fall like that, in such heavy amounts, with such clatter! And then I spend time in Delaware and Pennsylvania, and experience a rain-storm. Better still, I throw on my running gear and go out and *really experience* a rainstorm. The intense lash of it! Along the pavement-less street towards the woods, a hundred stagehands chasing me around with their twenty-five-litre buckets, drenching me and re-drenching me all over again until I can barely open my eyes. My clothes heavy and misshapen, slapping and wrapping and sticking. The trees offer a respite peppered with frequent ha-ha-look-at-you dousings from rain-heavy branches, and the river when I get there is swollen and crashing and bouncing around, jumping its leash, snapping and snarling, beautifully.

A decade earlier, it was mid-winter and we were visiting relatives in Plainfield, Vermont, right up there below the Canadian border. I'd visited in summer and had a rough and ready idea of the lie of the land, the forest tracks and swimming ponds, small-town wooden houses and backwoods corner stores that double up as video hire outlets and petrol stations. This December was different. We were staying in a small log cabin about five miles out of town and up, up, up in the forest. We arrived in the evening, it had been snowing for two months already and the car had chained wheels to get us there. The whole world fantastically white in the car's headlights. I was already looking forward to the following morning, wrapping up warmly and running on the cross-country ski paths. We watched a video of *The Odd Couple* on a TV set that couldn't receive TV programmes, while, outside, it carried on snowing.

In the morning I was up bright and early, changing into just about all the running clothes I'd brought with me – thermal base-layer, shirt, fleece, cagoule, running tights, gloves, balaclava – sweating already while still only half dressed. I opened the door and escaped. Outside, it was 17° below freezing and my breath immediately gathered and stuck to my balaclava like the dregs of a misshapen ice lolly. I crunched through the snow, my eyelids brittle and icy within the first minute of running. The running wasn't actually running – I clambered through drifts, each step laden with the clinging, leaden white stuff. The part of my balaclava protecting my mouth became brittle and stiff and began to thicken and sag with the ice. I loved it, though, all of it – the discomfort of it and the ridiculousness of it, me in the Vermont forests trying to run, the sight and sounds and smell of it all. Wonderful. Ten minutes and I was already incredibly cold. Within half an hour I had to beat a retreat, laughing at myself.

10

Three months into my stay in America and I'm now familiar with the series of barely connected footpaths that lead away from the house we're renting and down to a small wooded river valley. Any stretch of grass is fair game; garden verges and pebbled alleyways, close-cropped lawns and overgrown wasteland, anything but the unforgiving tarmac and concrete. The roads around here – and seemingly anywhere outside the cities – are obviously designed and built without pedestrians in mind; even a stretch of paved sidewalk is a godsend which can, at any given point, disappear to make way for a turning lane. This is car country. I'm reminded at every intersection of Heathcote Williams' *Autogeddon*, a snarling prose-poem in which aliens who might somehow hover watchfully above our planet could be forgiven for believing that cars are the dominant life form, and human beings only some kind of walking fuel, gobbled up and spat out of vehicles as and when required.

When forced by limited choice into running on America's roads, I'm reminded by the oil-fuelled swagger of great, heaving, jacked-up 4x4 monsters just who's actually in charge here. So why on earth – to use an inappropriate phrase – did the marathons move out of the parks and onto the roads? There's only one tenable reason: so that they could be bigger. A race in the quest for size, for the power of enormity, for the status that comes with weight of numbers. The 2010 New York City Marathon is the biggest marathon to date, and its 45,000 runners amount to more than half the population of Burnley. Imagine! As an event, as a spectacle, it's fascinating. As a mathematical equation, it's startling: a marathon runner takes around 41,000 steps to cover the 26.2 miles. That's 1,785,000 steps, collectively, in the space of a few hours. Picture the jarring impact of human muscle and bone against unyielding asphalt almost two million times and then add in the pollution (according to a study of air emissions in 1999, residents of Manhattan face the highest risk in the country of developing cancer from chemicals in the air) being breathed into each of those 45,000 pairs of lungs, and it begins to sound less like running and more like mass suicide. Maybe Jim Jones is manning one of the drinks stations, in charge of the Gatorade.

I had a favourite hill race, once. It was tucked away in the Calder Valley along the ridged, rutted boundary between Lancashire and Yorkshire, knotted into the raised grey twist of northern England's spine. It was called The Blue Pig Hill Race, and it was run from a tiny pub next to a densely forested river; the pub was called the Blue Pig, the entry fee was £1 and the first prize was a fluffy blue pig.

The first time I ran the race there were around sixty to seventy runners toeing the start line. Its eight-mile course around the fells and valleys scrambled and wriggled up through wooded hillsides and down rough, fast descents, slithered along farmland tracks and walled stiles, tangled with a jumbled maze of desolate country and post-industrial agricultural landscape (with its unmoved and unmoving animal tenants, what Ted Hughes described memorably as 'England's sluttiest sheep') before returning to the Blue Pig. A glorious mixture of mud, wood and windswept farmland. The race was run in January, during the post-Christmas hangover, so it was surprising that the following year there were upwards of 200 runners. Another couple of years later and we lined up in that field next to the pub, shivering in the frost, over 500 of us. Thin pathways were throttled with heaving runners, sheeptrods became muddied motorways and the race became a game of follow-my-leader. It became too big for its own good, and was humanely put down for its own good, never to be run again.

Wanting everything to be bigger – and measuring success in terms of size – holds no appeal to me at all. Where's the fun in watching a band's lead singer on a giant screen from a distance of several hundred yards? In what way is a car better simply because it's as long as a bus and has wheels the size of a small house? During the year or two after Chumbawamba had our one major hit single, we were constantly asked in interviews how we viewed our recent 'success'. The simple act of having been in a cooperatively run band for over a decade, doing something we loved, touring the world several times over and getting paid for enjoying ourselves – without having a hit record – wasn't counted as a success. Only a placing in the sales charts mattered. This is how we measure the world: in numbers, big numbers. ING, sponsors of the New York City Marathon, surely welcome the race's increasing size as much as they welcome their own total asset figure of $1.6 trillion. Some more, random figures for the race:

over 105,000 entrants compete in a lottery system for the 45,000 slots, while more than 6,000 volunteers participate on race day (along with the 100 full-time all-year-round organizers). The Marathon Eve Dinner feeds 15,000 marathoners and their guests 6,840 pounds of pasta, 1,800 pounds of salad, 15,000 apples and 18,000 cans of light beer (!). At the starting line there are 1,450 portable toilets, and pre-race food consumption includes 30,000 PowerBars, 90,000 bottles of water and 40,000 cups of coffee. During the race, volunteers hand out 62,370 gallons of water and 32,040 gallons of Gatorade in 2,250,000 paper cups while 80 photographers snap upwards of 1,000,000 photos of racers. And the 41 medical aid stations along the way are outfitted with over five tons of ice, 13,475 adhesive bandages and 390 tubs of Vaseline. Numbers upon numbers upon numbers.

'Any intelligent fool can make things bigger and more complex . . . it takes a touch of genius and a lot of courage to move in the opposite direction.' (Albert Einstein)

All this – two and a quarter million paper cups! – seems so far removed from the running that I know and love. Running that affirms life and melds with the earth beneath our feet. Running that confirms our connection to the world, away from the rounded-up, congregated, corralled and herded mass. Running that allows us to use our imagination.

Somewhere on that series of barely connected footpaths that lead away from the house we're renting and down to a small wooded river valley, my thoughts begin to stray along one or another half-concealed ideas, trailing off, opening out, leading somewhere or nowhere. How could they not, down here in this mess of constantly changing beauty? Our thoughts aren't linear and cordoned off, taped and channelled. To coin a delightful description of wildness by Jay Griffiths, they *wiggle*. Thoughts misbehave. They go wrong. Thoughts follow their noses, not the footsteps of the person in front. They satisfy their curiosity, they poke around, they wander.

Down here, less than a stone's throw from the houses and roads, the river is full to bursting with boulders and rocks, age-old and volcanic, clear water rushing in and around and between the huge, smoothed grey stones, looking like so many cracked dinosaur eggs. The river winds and turns and splits into two, or three, or branches right off; and here's where I go river-running, every dry morning, thin-soled running shoes feeling the angles and edges of the boulders, skipping and stepping and clambering along the river without falling in. Once, I try to run the river after a heavy rainfall, the rocks green and shining. I skid comically from the first slimy rocks, standing there in the freezing river laughing at myself and wiping the blood oozing from my elbow.

It's not sponsored or televised, but it's all fun. All this tripping over tree roots and not knowing precisely where I'm going and falling like a clown into rivers. But it is, I swear – it's fun. It's not (as some have described it) like going back to being a child again, as if in regression. It's just that the natural, exuberant, no-holds-barred playfulness we have as humans is educated out of us as we get older, squeezed out by convention and responsibility. Responsibility! Our first responsibility must surely be to enjoy ourselves. To have our children see us enjoying ourselves, so they might grow up thinking that, yes, life is a quest for joy, not a set pattern of inhibitions and denials. Adults, scared of looking foolish, won't even run for a bus they're about to miss. Somehow, as we grew older, running became silly, part of a job lot of joys and pleasures that, as we turn from kids to adults, we're supposed to tie up in a big hessian sack and throw into the nearest canal, where they can sink with a splash, a glug and a muffled yelp.

Of course, running being so perfect an exercise (and so perfect for exercising), so humanly primal and natural, we've invented a safely regulated version of its former, excitable and celebratory self – and we've created an industry to support and coordinate it, to supervise, measure and classify it. An industry of big boasts, big sponsors and ever bigger numbers. And how lucky that we've also got the patronage of multi-national clothing and footwear companies to try to make this regulated version of running that bit more comfortable with their breathable, cushioned, flexible, moisture-wicking, odour-fighting products; that we've got the patronage of multi-billionaire financial service salesmen to sponsor our run along the demarcated, imagination-free confines of the city marathon.

The geometric system of urban planning – setting out city streets according to a grid – was, from the beginning, a means by which a ruler or government could impose order. The system of 'blocks', with its intersections, straight lines and repeated patterns demonstrated the imposition of a ruler's will; proof that discipline and conformity could dominate the natural, add-on, radial (and plain old weird) way we live our lives.

Straight lines represent order. Modern cities have often

been designed around specific military, religious or political ideas, all three of which tend to revel in conformist rigidity and a sense of structure inherited from ideas of grandeur and imposition. Long, wide ceremonial routes fit for military parades crop up in cities all over the world – Berlin, Mexico City, Oslo, Paris, St Petersburg, Vienna, Washington, DC. Brasilia, purpose-built to be Brazil's capital city, was constructed explicitly on the pattern of a huge cross. From as long ago as the Renaissance, grid systems began to dominate urban planning, specifically in cities. Older cities are now recognizable for their organic, flowing shapes, dead ends, twisting roadways, thoroughfares that follow rivers and valleys rather than impose themselves upon (and in defiance of) the natural topography of the land.

The gradual straightening of our city's roads was further quickened – the creative architect's fanciful digressions ironed out and flattened – by the advent of motor traffic. Modern cities are planned not around the changing, evolving inconsistencies of people but around the rigidity of the car. Left turn, right turn, straight ahead. Parts of many American cities boldly ignore the idea of pedestrian travel altogether, eliminating pavements on the assumption that no one would ever want to walk when we all have the luxury of our air-conditioned, faux-leather-upholstered, automatic-locking, crumple-zoned, airbagged dream machines. (And, should you ever feel the need to visit the countryside and drive across a ploughed field, they'll provide you with 4-wheel drive, too.)

It's in this accentuated grid system, so perfect for quelling public order and able to accommodate the easy movement of armoured vehicles, that we choose to run our marathons. Right there, in the very heart of Autogeddon. For half a day in the year, cars are banished to the driveways and double garages, the streets flung open to the people. For half a day every year, runners can ignore the Walk signs and instead laugh in apparent irony at the Don't Walk signs. They can weave in and out of lanes, charge right through the pedestrian crossings, follow the white lines and vomit in the gutters and grates. Look at a map of the New York City Marathon, run your finger along the route from Staten Island to Manhattan and finally to Central Park. The route is a frightening series of long, straight lines, an Etch-A-Sketch charge along the city's main arteries with as few turns as possible, terminating with a short and final death rattle of small bends as it enters the park. The runners, that thirty-abreast juggernaut of flesh and blood-aching bones, thumbs its nose at car culture with all the defiance of a lobster in a pan of not-yet-boiled water. Yes, the marathon runners can have the city and its gridded strictness for half a day – but, believe me, the city will take it back as soon as the sweat dries on those silver space blankets.

11

'Running's always been a big thing in our family, especially running away from the police.'

(Alan Sillitoe, *The Loneliness of the Long Distance Runner*)

Nineteen seventy-three, in a classroom full of flared trousers and feather cuts, grey jumpers, scruffy blazers and blue school ties. Ivy Bank Secondary Modern was part of a rolling government experiment in education, a mixed-up version of supposedly socialist teaching that was intended to cut out exaggerated 'streaming', a throw-'em-all-in-together jumble of skewed thinking. There was still streaming, it was just less obvious than the previous 11-plus system, where children were ruthlessly graded, selected and divided on the results of one nationwide examination taken by all eleven-year-olds. The teachers at Ivy Bank were pulled this way and that trying to accommodate the keen, the lazy, the troublemakers and the swots, knowing there was a hush-hush 'R' unit – R for Remedial, for the rubbish, for the rejected – situated in a makeshift holding unit around the back of the school building.

It was into this atmosphere of muddle and jumble that my English teacher handed out tatty copies of Alan

Sillitoe's book of short stories, *The Loneliness of the Long Distance Runner*. First published in 1959, the collection was headed by the title story that, over the next couple of schooldays, threatened to shift the way I thought; about rebellion, about writing and about running. Sillitoe was one of the 'Angry Young Men', a bandied together group of writers who wrote about the British class system in the language of its protagonists – in dialect, rough-edged, with fights, sex and swearing. His heroes were flawed rebels who dodged their way through his stories without the Hollywood makeovers of James Dean or Marlon Brando. Sillitoe's leading men were definitely, defiantly uncool; they were scruffy, unfocused, funny, sometimes pathetic, and, most importantly of all, they were *a bit like us*. Or like the blokes we thought we wanted to be. Rebels with causes – the causes being youth, class and *where you're from*. Alf Tupper for grown-ups.

In 'The Loneliness of the Long Distance Runner', Colin Smith (an everyday name for the everyman) is convicted of robbery and sent to a juvenile detention centre, where he discovers a talent for cross-country running. The narrative – young man robs factory, gets caught, gets sent down and is offered early release if he can win the Blue Riband Cup against the neighbouring private school cross-country team – is pinned together with the mud, trees and trails of Smith's early-morning runs, wheezing, frost-edged sprints punctuated by first-person blasts against the authorities that put Smith where he is. It's a tale without a fairy-tale ending (in fact, in the humdrum universe of the English Literature lesson – Thursday afternoons, three hours without a break – the ending came as a complete

61

shock to all of us). And suddenly, running was counted in with the accumulation of stuff that I was beginning to stockpile on my side, on the side that's clever, interesting, thoughtful, inspiring and, above all for this 12-year-old schoolboy back then, different.

So as soon as I tell myself I'm the first man ever to be dropped into the world, and as soon as I take that first flying leap out into the frosty grass of an early morning when even birds haven't the heart to whistle, I get to thinking, and that's what I like. I go my rounds in a dream, turning at lanes or footpath corners without knowing I'm turning, leaping brooks without knowing they're there, and shouting good morning to the early cow-milker without seeing him. It's a treat, being a long-distance runner, out in the world by yourself with not a soul to make you bad-tempered or tell you what to do or that there's a shop to break and enter a bit back from the next street. Sometimes I think that I've never been so free as during that couple of hours when I'm trotting up the path out of the gates and turning by that barefaced, big-bellied oak tree at the lane end.

It's a good life, I'm saying to myself, if you don't give in to coppers and Borstal-bosses and the rest of them bastard-faced In-laws. Trot-trot-trot. Puff-puff-puff. Slap-slap-slap go my feet on the hard soil. Swish-swish-swish as my arms and side catch the bare branches of a bush.

Of course there were other books that fired my imagination, and it wasn't long before I discovered a whole world of clever, thoughtful, provocative writers – poets, drama-tists, journalists, agitators and myth-makers, historians

62

and ranters, polemicists and pamphleteers. But for that time in 1979, and I'm sure long past the time when I'm a 50-year-old man beating my own paths through the woods and fields, this short tale of the boy who runs as his own sweating, gritted-teeth metaphor for *beating the bastards* is one of the best things I'm ever likely to read.

What the story taught me, captivated and inspired by this thumbed, grubby schoolbook, is that rebels don't always wear leather jackets and mumble; that writers can write in the dialect of our class and our culture; and that running, at least the kind of running that Sillitoe describes, this country running where the slap-slap-slap of your feet matches the buzz-buzz-buzz of your thinking, sounds like fun! I'd always loved sport, especially football, and it was around this time – moving into bigger schools with a bigger pool of good footballers – that I understood that, no, I'd never make it as a professional footballer. That I'd better start thinking about other career options, since playing outside-right for Burnley Football Club probably wasn't going to be an option. And this lad in the book, he was obviously good – but he didn't care about winning races. He had bigger concerns, and he could use his running to say what he wanted to say.

I wanted to do that.

One year earlier, at Lowerhouse Junior School, in a class-room full of eleven-year-olds, our teacher – who was also in charge of physical education – gathered us together in the school hall. This mumbling old man, all kindly smile and unhealthy obsession with tradition, had been given the job of boys' games master without ever having to pull on a pair of training shoes. He was a frail, slight man who wore checked suits and delighted in correct enunciation *(E*nun`ci*a"tion)*. His party piece was reciting Noël Coward's 'Mad Dogs and Englishmen', which he'd deliver with unseemly dollops of Queen's Englishness, rolling his Rs for effect and flapping his arms theatrically. In fact his first lesson in PE at the start of the school year – knowing we'd all brought our football boots and kit – was to sit us down, clean the blackboard and teach us the proper positions of play on a cricket field. On subsequent rainy days, despite our eagerness to get out and slither around in the mud chasing a heavy leather ball, he insisted on us singing Gilbert & Sullivan operettas instead in the dry and fidgety classroom. (As a boy, that was unforgiveable. Even as an adult, I have never forgiven either him or Gilbert & Sullivan.)

So that day, in the school hall, he had us congregated in a semi-circle before instructing us that, having had notice of an inter-schools track and field athletics meeting, today we would have a trial run. This was to consist of two classes of boys and girls having a one-mile race around the local streets. He'd drawn a map, and pointed to the route with a wooden pointer: the same pointer he used to stab at Gilbert & Sullivan lyrics on a projected screen. None of us had ever raced formally before. We gathered in the school-yard and stood along a chalked line drawn on the ground. The teacher blew a whistle and off we went, badly shod and in football shirts or vests, running like idiots around the streets of Lowerhouse. Out of the gates, along Kiddrow Lane to the junction at the church, left along Padiham Road, left again down Lowerhouse Lane and follow it back to the school.

I won the race, easily. I was shocked. I didn't know I

could run; actually, of course I knew I could run – but I didn't know I could run a race. And win! It didn't make up for missing a game of football, but I was chuffed and proud. The games teacher said nothing, but that was understandable – there was a mutual hatred at play, me of his bloody operettas and him of me. The next week he pinned up on the noticeboard a list of competitors for the inter-schools track and field competition. And there was my name – not chosen to run the 800 metres, the 1,500 metres or the two-mile cross-country but to do the long jump. I'd never done the long jump in my life! Now all I could do was wait around for a year or so in my under-sized gym shorts waiting for Alan Sillitoe to turn up.

In his book *The Runner's Guide to the Meaning of Life*, Amby Burfoot expounds eloquently on the old 'running is a metaphor for life' theme before straying awkwardly into a dismissive swipe at Sillitoe's short story. His thumbnail summary of the tale as a boy using running to express defiance is brought to a breathless halt by a declaration of 'enough already'. Running, says Burtroot, is about community, not isolation.

Despite completely misreading the nature of Sillitoe's leading character (he doesn't run to express defiance at all – he runs for the chance to leave the prison buildings behind for an hour every morning, runs to think and plan, runs for the love of running; the defiance is not in Smith's running but in his refusal to win a race for the governor) Burfoot is right to see runners as a community. In a fractured and isolating world, participating in sport remains one of the great reasons to gather and to share, to make links. Our ancient communities based around family,

65

neighbourhood, church and work have less of a hold on us now as communication and transport keep us physically separate.

One of the reasons my family and I are spending time in Arden, Delaware, is because this is a place built historically and politically on a real and tangible notion of community. Arden was founded in 1900 by socialist tax reformers who wanted to retain economic and social control over the way they live. They bought land, cultivated it, and spent pleasure-seeking summers and long, hard winters building their own homes, often living for years under canvas. What they built was a township that has retained a degree of control over its own affairs; it is regulated by frequent town meetings at which all residents have an equal vote. There are weekly communal dinners, long-standing associations (or 'gilds') that take care of everything from the road signs to the kids' summer camp, and people-driven statutes that promote neighbourliness and a fierce communality. Arden has been a home and a resting place for great writers, thinkers and artists (including the novelist Upton Sinclair) as well as homebuilders, carpenters, printers and inventors. In short, it's a living, working community that I haven't experienced anywhere else I've lived.

I am also part of an international community of artists, writers, film-makers and musicians with whom I've struck up links over the past thirty years – a loose congregation of people who share ideas and collaborate on an ad-hoc basis. Being part of that community is a privilege; when I see old photographs of artists having huge picnics on French riverbanks – Marcel Duchamp in cravat and pinstripes, reaching for the fruit jam, a bow-tied George Grosz smiling for the camera, Kurt Schwitters' kids playing in the background – I feel that I'm part of a tradition of communities based on nothing less than ideas. We don't have mass picnics of course (more's the pity if you ask me. Pass the jam sandwiches), but the day-to-day exchange of craft and opinion is as important a community as I can imagine.

And then there's the running community, that strangely shaped huddle fuelled on shared experience, on races won and lost, on expectation, disappointment and ambition. It's a strange community that is often turned defiantly inwards, away from the world – for many runners this is the space to get away from work, from financial or relationship problems, from daily boredom and powerlessness. But it's more than a community of escapologists; it thrives not so much on what we say but on what we do. Sometimes, when running with a group of club runners, the hill-repeats session can be so hard, so intense, that there's very little conversation. It doesn't matter; there's a shared experience, a gaspingly physical relationship. Sometimes, too, there are long, winding summer runs filled with constant chatter, open, easy conversation born of a huge sky and an easy pace.

Talking while running isn't like talking in the boardroom or canteen. It's driven by changing landscape, for one thing – following a thread of banter leading somehow from the view over a glacial U-shaped valley to the best way to catch an egg at the annual Burnsall Village Fair. Some runners are incessant natterers, some barely say a word. Some will take a moorland run as an open invitation to put the world to rights. Some will just look around, drink it all in, and pause on the hour to spit out 'bloody hell. Look at that' before setting off again into a breathy, puff-puff quiet. Some, on group runs, will take up the challenge of making fun of everyone, inventing nicknames and peppering jokes with put-downs and impersonations. Some see running as a time and space to creakily open up the safety valve to the sorrows and sadnesses that stay hidden the rest of the time. Some use running to talk about the land under their feet, the flowers, trees, birds, cloud formations; the history of a place, its geography and geology.

I began to run on the fells in the late 1980s knowing only the side of running that is isolated, self-determined and deeply personal. This wasn't a team game, it was about my relationship with my own body, with what I could make it do. The camaraderie and spirit of running as a communal sport came as a surprise; here was a bunch of people of various ages and backgrounds who, on the face of it, had very little in common. The running, I discovered, was reason enough for community. Being squeezed into the back of a small windowless work van with six other runners, scattered cushions for seats and frequent stops to combat car-sickness on a four-hour journey to run on the Welsh mountains, convinced me of that spirit of togetherness. In 1990 our small local running club – Pudsey & Bramley – became British fell-running champions, not least because we engendered a ridiculously tight comradeship, encouraged each other, and treated the serious business of running up and down Britain's biggest mountains as a year-long excuse to have fun, together.

There are relay races held every few months around the hills and valleys of northern England, six- or seven-hour circular routes run by teams of ten or twelve, in pairs. Team selection for these relay races is crucial; pairings have to match as closely as possible. Despite this, in every pair there's often one runner stronger than the other – and suddenly the faster runner is faced with a problem encompassing the very essence of human nature. Does that runner exploit a ruthless self-centredness or submit to the demands of the wider community? Does the runner leave the slower partner struggling several hundred yards behind, thus making it clear to spectators and team-mates just who was fastest on the day, or do the pair work together, the faster runner slowing up to encourage and embolden the slower of the two? It's surprising how many runners will, in fact, leave their struggling partners behind – significantly, not in running clubs that seem to foster a genuine team spirit. There's a place for focused, self-centred individualism in running, but when it's most appealing is when it runs alongside a selfless communality.

But running isn't, in general, a team sport. It doesn't fall prey to the well-worn homilies we all heard from gym teachers in school (*'Individually, we are one drop. Together, we are an ocean.'*) And it doesn't, for the most part, rely on coaches and managers. In fact, one of the great things about running is that there isn't anyone telling you what to do. When I run with other people, I tend to run behind them. I prefer it that way; I prefer to let them lead. I feel like I've spent a lot of my time in Chumbawamba, thousands of meetings and rehearsals, trying to drive ideas, working to make something happen, pushing towards conclusions and agreements. So running with someone is a perfect time to follow. I like watching someone else's feet in front of me – as long as I can see those feet out of the corner of my eye, I can allow my mind to wander upwards and outwards and away from the ground. It's a privilege.

12

Danger, and fear of danger, holds a special place in our twenty-first-century urban lives. We scare ourselves half to death, restrict ourselves, create irrational panic and invent imaginary enemies. Fear is a controller. If you stick to the main road, you'll be safe. If you run down that alleyway and head off into the woods – well, there could be anything down there. The unknown. The question mark. Fortunately we have people who have our best interests at heart, people who will protect us from this scary, unknown stuff. They'll categorize that stuff, and fence off that stuff, and they'll fight that stuff until it pleads for mercy (and sell you the insurance cover).

City marathon running is an expression of our fear of the unknown and our willingness to collaborate in our own confinement. Marathon running celebrates the thrill of mass participation, but at a cost of losing a sense of our place in the world. Is this the culmination of all that physical effort, the training and planning, the sheer hard work – to pad along in a regulated, cordoned-off procession? I'm not pooh-poohing the joy of the get-together, the mob, the street party; even as I write this I remember football matches, concerts, parties where I've been filled with the head-bursting intensity of that spirit of congregation. The mass,

71

amassed, singing, playing and baying. A demonstration in Genoa, running with the crowd. Wembley Stadium, chorusing with 40,000 football fans. Festival marquees, dancing, surrounded by others dancing, dancing, dancing. There's a power in numbers that, when we experience it, thrills us, brings a surge of body electricity, a tingling, a welling up, sensing our small part in something so big. Marathon running, if only by sheer numerical weight, strives to capture this feeling. It's a huge party – look at the costumes, the face paint, the hand-made signs (in case I'm on the telly!). And at the start at least, it's all smiles and waves and *look, Mummy, the Circus is coming to town!*

I don't begrudge anyone's big party, least of all one that displaces the everyday non-stop humdrum bark and squeal of traffic for a short while. What I wonder, though, is firstly whether this has much to do with running. How it connects with the primal, simple beauty of moving quickly across the earth, naturally and easily. And secondly I wonder how we've come to accept that the pinnacle of this act of running is to allow ourselves to be corralled, fenced in and directed; that while we're busy being cheered on and revelling in that massed spirit, we're not noticing how much we're being enclosed, cut off from the world, by an overbearing and domineering superstructure.

Are we so petrified by the pathways outside the marathon route? Are we really prepared to let other people tell us where we ought to be running? Henry David Thoreau says it beautifully, in his essay 'Walking':

The most alive is the wildest. Not yet subdued to man, its presence refreshes him. One who pressed forward incessantly,

and never rested from his labours, who grew fast and made
infinite demands on life, would always find himself in a
new country or wilderness, and surrounded by the raw
material of life. He would be climbing over the prostrate
stems of primitive forest-trees.

There it is, ready to break free of the paragraph, that one phrase 'made infinite demands on life'. Make demands! Somewhere, amid the communal partying and singing, our nature insists that we make demands. Running off the beaten track – or, rather, off the black-topped highway – is a way of making those demands. Overcoming the over-bearing sense of fear that we're inheriting. Don't climb trees, you might fall and break your leg. Don't touch that, it might snap in your hands. Don't break the rules, you might be sued. Thoreau's cry of resistance is that there is little to fear in the things we don't know. Climb the pros-trate stems of primitive trees, seize that part of life that isn't given to you in a tastefully wrapped package.

It doesn't have to stop there, of course. The 'raw material of life' extends into the everyday, into our work and our homes, as well as our leisure. Everything's a route choice. I met a man at a race recently, a man who I hadn't seen for over fifteen years. In the meantime, as he described it, he'd 'got married, got two children, got fat and got divorced'. He was piecing things back together now, taking on ten-mile forest races and thoroughly enjoying himself in a new rela-tionship. He'd claimed he'd originally got married and ended up in a place he dreaded, 'wearing khakis and chinos'. Sometimes relationships end, sadly, badly, but often for the better. Life turns corners, offers possibilities, tells you that you don't have to stay on that straight and narrow trudge up Manhattan's First Avenue. Relationship, divorce, children, they're all turning points, places where you get a chance to change where you're going.

With a month-old boy and an 8-year-old daughter in tow, my partner Casey and I have headed across the Atlantic for a year to shake life up a bit, to take a risk, to have an adventure. It's not to everyone's liking – you don't have to transplant your whole life somewhere else to prove you can deal with change. When I left school I chose to try art college because I wanted that adventure; I then left university within a year in search of adventure; joined a band, spent ten years in the back of transit vans with very little money, for adventure. I don't know if I've always made those 'infinite demands on life', but I've tried to ensure I don't get mired in the warm coziness of complacency; or, worse, the boredom of repetition. There's a song by Manchester band The Fall, the same two chords backwards and forwards over a clanging beat, their version of 'the three Rs', 'Repetition, repetition, repetition . . .', and I can hear it now, as I write, and I can soundtrack that repeating line to a close-up of 45,000 pairs of feet slap-slap-slapping through sticky pools of Gatorade on tarmac.

My grandma and grandad lived the last few years of their lives in an added-on bit of my mum's house in Burnley. When my grandma became infirm, it was left to my grandad to do the weekly shopping. Together they'd fuss around their little flat, making sure he had enough shopping bags, gathering coupons snipped from the local newspaper, hunting for the car keys. Then my grandad, wrapped up against the inclement weather (whatever the season), would drive at a stately 15 mph down the main dual carriageway into the town centre and disappear for two hours making sure he bought everything on the list. The list was sacrosanct. To deviate from the list was to call into question the very foundation of a secure and happy life.

After hospitalization for recurring illnesses, my grandad died in 2004, my grandma less than a year later. They were both lovely people, and the security and love they gave me were never dependent on my sticking to some pre-arranged life path (I think my grandad genuinely enjoyed my early infatuation with Alice Cooper, however much he protested). After they died, going through their various belongings, my dad made a discovery in the part of the garage they'd used as storage space; it was filled with new and unopened boxes of cornflakes and tea, tins of soup and beans, wraps of butter and jars of instant coffee. We worked out that they'd been using the same shopping list every week, irrespective of what they needed or had enough of; yes, there are thirty-five tins of oxtail soup in the garage, but it's on the list – look! – so into the shopping basket it went. Like many older people, they feared change. They needed safeguards and guarantees, something to rely on; those old worn slippers, they're more than tatty footwear, they're reminders of who we are and where we are.

The reason I suddenly head off in the direction of stories about my grandma and grandad is because I want to remind myself that even though, as an almost-fifty-year-old, I should be jogging gratefully towards that garageful of tins and packets, with as much grace as I can muster – instead I'm out in the woods and hills every day running the miles, wrapping up in winter and being the first to make footprints in the frost, dreaming of trails, routes, mud, sunsets and sunrises. If it all looks like a savage self-denial, then I hold my hands up. Maybe it is. But what I fear more than change – what really scares me – is not changing. Of getting stuck. There's an old Chinese proverb: 'The only one to like change is a baby.' I think that's rubbish, frankly; I think we can teach ourselves not just to like but to love change, however old we are. Every day, out in the world somewhere, tripping over broken tree branches and crossing swollen rivers, guessing what might be under leaf fall and watching foxes dive for cover, I look at the way things change right in front of me. Even after all these years, it's all still a guessing game, a wonderful jump into the dark.

Whenever I'm tempted to complain about post-race cuts and bruises, or of being too tired to get out and run, or of simply being too old to be out hacking my way through unknown forests and leaping from stone to stone across a fast-flowing river, I have Henry Miller in my ear, and he's rapping over The Fall's 'Repetition', telling me that a man who yearns for security – for what's safe – is a man who'd '. . . chop off his limbs in order to have artificial ones which will give him no pain or trouble'.

13

The first marathon runner, the man who started the whole thing, was a messenger called Phidippides. The story as it's passed down, from around 500 BC, part myth, part fact and part clever storytelling, tells that Phidippides was ordered to carry the news from the battlefield at Marathon to Athens – twenty-five miles away – that the Persians were attacking Greece. Some accounts talk of Phidippides having already run 150 miles in the two days prior to this. Depending on which version of the story you believe, his message either called for reinforcements or announced a Greek victory. The latter records his words upon reaching Athens as 'We have won'. Whereupon the knackered Phidippides collapsed and died on the spot from exhaustion.

In homage, the first modern Olympics, held in Athens in 1896, featured a version of this run, set at a distance of just under twenty-five miles. Despite various versions of the marathon being run at subsequent Olympic Games, it wasn't until the London Olympics of 1908 that the race's length was standardized, though the farcical reason for the distance being set at 26.2 miles bears closer inspection. Originally designed as a twenty-five-mile race, the Olympic Marathon was lengthened by a mile at the request of King Edward VII in order for it to begin at the private East Terrace of Windsor Castle, so that the royals (bless 'em) could have an exclusive view of the start unhindered by the 'public'.

Shortly before the Games opened it was realized that the royal entrance to the White City Stadium (used exclusively by the blue bloods and their carriages) could not be used for the runners as the marathon entrance – it was raised to permit easy descent by the royal party from their carriages, and so did not open onto the track – so an alternative entrance was chosen, diagonally opposite the royal box. The distance to the stadium remained twenty-six miles and the finishing line was left unchanged; but in order that the royal spectators, including Queen Alexandra, could have the perfect view of the final yards, the direction of running around the track was changed to an unprecedented clockwise. This meant that the total distance became 26 miles 385 yards. Considering the inconvenience she'd caused, it was fitting that Queen Alexandra enjoyed the spectacle of little Dorando Pietri being helped across the finishing line in a state of confusion and collapse, the supporting arms of officials being enough to disqualify him from winning the race. Despite his official DNF status (Did Not Finish – the runner's mark of Cain), the Queen presented him the following day with a special silver cup. See, he was a winner after all.

In the big city marathons, everyone's a winner. Five, six, nine hours to finish the race, it's still faster than reading a self-help book. Running along city streets surrounded by well-wishers and punctuated by drinks stations, we can be forgiven for thinking we've conquered our own personal

Everest, reached our particular North Pole. And it *is* a fantastic achievement, to get all those thousands of people off their couches and into running shoes. To turn self-deprecating losers (not my description – read the blogs and post-race accounts) into winners.

Here's an extract from a book by John Bingham, *The Courage to Start*:

> *Seven and a half hours after I started, I finished. I crossed the finish line, sat down, and began to sob. It was not an ordinary cry of relief, or sorrow, or even joy. This pain was not coming from my body. These tears were not just from this day. These were tears born of a lifetime of failing.*
>
> *I cried for the six-year-old who couldn't run as fast as the others. I cried for the twelve-year-old who couldn't hit the ball or catch like the others. I cried for all the times I stood alone . . . for the teenager who knew nothing about life and for the young man who knew nothing about love.*
>
> *My wife came to meet me and I looked up and said to her: 'It's such a long way. Such a long, long way.' I'm sure she thought I meant the course. I didn't. I meant that it is such a long way for many of us to travel before we find ourselves.*

Is this what it's really all about, another branch of the Positive Thinking juggernaut? Are we celebrating Phidippides, collapsed and dying, plucky do-or-(literally)-die hero? Are we so desperate to project onto that dull, baking tarmac our life's quest for self-discovery that we turn the beautiful, natural pleasure of running, free and unbridled, into a procession of self-revealing insights and soul-searching? One inevitable result of this amalgamation of the marathon distance with the murky business of 'finding ourselves' is that the character of the race has changed for the better. Post-race newspapers report the eighty-two-year-olds, the heart attacks, the celebrity joggers, while the winners barely get a mention. And as the popularity of marathons has increased, the speed of the race has slowed to its current snail's pace. In 1980, the average finish time for a male marathoner was 3.32 hours, according to *Running USA*. Today, it's more than 4.20. In 2003, the start time of the New York City Marathon was moved forward an hour to grant thousands of stragglers extra hours so they could finish before sunset. Despite the big city marathons paying out vast sums to top athletes in appearance fees (which in many cases are bigger than the winning purse – the spectacle trumps the racing) the sheer weight of numbers has changed the nature of the marathon, to the point where it's barely a race at all. When Dorando Pietri was disqualified as he crossed that finish line in London (who remembers the actual victor?) he kick-started an industry. A business. Everyone's A Winner, Inc. He wasn't to know, but he took the baton from Phidippides and (as they say) ran with it. Since then a thousand shoe company entrepreneurs, self-help gurus, professional fitness fanatics and believers in the American dream have helped to create a race that's so big, so popular, that it threatens all other forms of running with extinction.

14

I'm standing at the junction of Brooklyn's Fourth Avenue and 95th Street, looking northwards. This is one of the straightest sections of the New York City Marathon, almost four miles of four-lane blacktop right the way down to 1st Street and beyond – over a hundred blocks. The runners, barely two miles into the race, pour off the Verrazano-Narrows Bridge, filtering towards the hum of police motorcycles and between the cordoned-off avenue of traffic cones. There's POLICE DO NOT CROSS tape lining the road and the whole route is blocked to traffic for one block on both sides of the course. The band in front of the Yamaha dealership turn the volume up, and up, and up, growling their way through the Delta blues in a way only middle-aged white men can – they chug chug chug, take solos, grimace and play call-and-response with the small crowd gathered outside Dunkin' Donuts. Spectators clutch coffee mugs, ready to yell when the mad parade arrives. Go, Brad! Good job, Lucy!

The New Yorkers are used to their marathon; one Sunday a year they get to come out and watch the parade, arching their eyebrows at some of the running outfits and whooping at the occasional octogenarian. They all want to see the rescued Chilean miner, but nobody seems to know what he looks like. Dunkin' Donuts are milking the marathon for all it's worth, giving out free placards and selling doughnuts and brand-emblazoned woolly hats from a trestle table on the pavement. There's a man dressed as a doughnut chatting to a woman dressed as a coffee cup; they're probably worried that a sweet-toothed giant might sweep down and carry them off. Suddenly, a commotion: several police cars and the leading runners are here and gone so fast (somewhere between the band's middle eight and second guitar solo) they barely raise a cheer; *Look!* I want to shout – *That was Haile Gebrselassie!* But it's a chilly morning in Brooklyn, and most of the people are watching the woman dressed as a coffee cup dancing to the blues band across the street.

Below me the subway rattles and hisses on its way from the station at 87th Street, the trickle of runners becomes a stream and then a tide, and the band have now (apparently) got their mojo workin'. A woman holds up a sign, KIRSTEN YOU GO GIRL, holds it up high above her head, wondering if she'll have to keep it there for the two hours it takes her friend to pass this spot. 'Follow the blue line!' a shout from one of the runners. There's a broken blue line painted along the entire course, the shortest route, the 26.2, the line to fix on. It divides the roadway like an invitation to CUT HERE, and all the while the blues band are reminding me just why I don't listen to music while I'm running. We're four miles or so into the race and there's the occasional smile or wave; but even at this early stage the runners are settled into their rhythm, eyes focused on the heels of the runner in front, some already looking for a water station, a toilet or a place to dump that extra layer of clothing. As the sun rises, the runners liberally ditch their outer layers. The race is getting serious.

At this point there are clothes everywhere – discarded gloves, hats, sweat-tops, hoodies, jackets, tights – piled up at the sides of the street, being flung away in a steady cascade of abandoned moisture-wicking neolite and taped seam fino-tech material. This orgy of wastefulness would be more depressing were it not for volunteers collecting it after the race – over a ton of disposed running gear – and donating it to charity shops and Goodwill stores. How can so many people get their choice of clothing so wrong? I can't recall ever throwing away an item of clothing while out running. In the giant-sized carnival that is the New York City Marathon, within a few feet of the comfort zone of that broken blue line, there's a pack mentality that tells you that, yes, other people are throwing away perfectly good hats and tops and tights, and maybe I should do it, too, so that nobody thinks I'm weird.

That's the point of the city marathons, of course – safety in numbers. Nothing to fear, we're all in it together. Despite the crowds lining the streets, despite the bands playing and the cop sirens wailing, despite the cacophony going on around the runners, this is a buttoned-up world where everything bar that simple act of running is provided. Above the racket of the music and sandwiched between the tackiness of Dunkin' Donuts and those long, stretched lines of police tape, I sense only repetition and overcrowding – two words I'd associate more with a zoo than with running. Does the caged animal, padding softly and slowly in its circles, dream of the thrill of the chase?

15

In Burnley, the only running I ever did outside school was away from gangs of lads. Five o'clock on a Saturday evening, after watching Burnley FC at Turf Moor, a bunch of us would walk home up Manchester Road, along one of the steep sides of the town's natural bowl, to where we lived at the top of Rosehill – scattered between the fish 'n' chip shop, the Parklands housing estate and the farm at the end of our street, stranded there by urbanization. Being one of the country's northernmost football teams meant carloads of southbound visiting fans left town along that main Manchester Road, so as we walked we'd have to keep an eye out for trouble.

Sure enough, several times we'd be confronted by long-haired hooligans shouting abuse at us in cockney accents from car windows. If we'd played one of the bigger teams we'd have our Burnley scarves tucked out of sight and keep as low a profile as possible, four or five of us in our parka jackets and Dr Marten boots. If a car did come to a sudden halt beside us we'd run for our lives, scattering in all directions as older, seasoned yobs in unfeasibly huge flared jeans would jump from a battered Ford Escort (with its sun-visor reading 'Gaz' and 'Sharon') and chase us up and down the road while onlookers tut-tutted and wondered what the country was coming to. It wasn't unusual to climb garden fences and trample flowerbeds, half scared to death and half exhilarated by the adrenalin rush. A mate of ours in a brand-new three-quarter-length leather coat was once chased by bat-wielding Liverpool fans onto the nearby railway tracks and caught. You can't run in a coat that weighs half your own body weight and wraps itself around your legs if you attempt more than a shuffle. Not only did he get a beating, he had his coat stolen, too. Somewhere in Liverpool there's a 30-year-old coat hanging like a trophy in an ageing hooligan's wardrobe, a reminder of the good old days when these hard nuts could sport ridiculous haircuts, chant playground rhymes and kick the living daylights out of much younger adolescent kids with impunity. Some lads thought the honourable thing to do was to stand and fight (like a man, they might have drawled, but the accent didn't suit drawling) but my friends and me, we plumped for self-preservation over honour and learnt how to run. That was what running was for – avoiding a kicking. I never got caught.

Several years later I was actively involved in the so-called 'punk wars', when for the crime of wearing zips and pins on your jacket and having cropped hair you could be chased across town by over-ripe Teddy boys or pimply Mods. The Mods, who gave me a particularly long and exhausting run through the streets of the gentle south-east town of Maidstone (where I spent three months studying art) were at least, to their credit, able to muster a fierce jog despite wearing huge green coats with voluminous hoods. The Teds, on the other hand, were particularly pathetic – all indolent beer bellies and receding duck's arse haircuts

– and never stood a chance wearing crepe-soled brothel creepers. They didn't so much run as wobble. Had they taken the time to change into their Hi-Tec Silver Shadows before giving chase, I might now proudly bear the fading scars of an overheated cultural exchange.

16

I write this while I'm running. Each chapter of this book has played and replayed itself in my head a hundred times, ideas and conclusions and questions all arguing with each other, bickering, taking me away from the here and now of a forest path or a rain-swept moor. I allow myself two ideas for each run, reduce them to key words, store them in my memory for later and then regain my focus on what's happening beneath my feet. It's hard for my mind not to wander, just as my feet desire to wander. I know from talking to other runners that this isn't abnormal, that everything we see, hear, smell and touch can spark off an exclamation, a question, a problem or an answer.

According to sports psychologists, there's a pattern to how we think when we run. Let's assume we're wound up, tired and full of the problems of work, family, money and chafing shorts. For the first ten minutes of a run these problems squat there, indolent, like Philip Larkin's toad, 'Its hunkers heavy as hard luck'. At this point in a run, I stop, stretch, look around. I learnt a while ago that pre-run stretching is less effective than stretches done when you're warmed up and loose – perfect, for this gives me a chance to draw a faint, dotted line under any unsolved problems before setting off again. During the next ten minutes the toad slinks off, replaced by some amount of coming-to-terms-with-everything, a bit of it-could-be-worse and gradually, sometimes, a deeply satisfying oh-that-must-be-the-solution. Heading towards half an hour and with the physical effort of a scramble, a trip, a steep ascent or a river crossing, my body releases the neurochemical endorphin into the brain, which famously helps to blank out physical pain and results in what is known as 'runner's high'. From thirty minutes onwards I'll experience a sense of relative 'oneness' with my surroundings, becoming less cynical, less angry, less self-deprecating. I don't have to lose my sense of critical judgement or my ability to understand danger (especially from my surroundings), but I can come to understand both the thrill of running and the sense of wellbeing I can bring to the rest of my life, feeling that I've learnt something from the world, from the experience of being in the world.

It sounds like another commercial for self-help therapy, of course, but in this case I'm not learning from a bearded guru or a cheerleading Texan millionaire; I'm learning from nature, learning by experience and by instinct. I learn by paying attention to it; there's very little 'switching off' in wild running. Switch off and you might end up face down in the mud. This morning, on a wet and sludgy run along the Brandywine River, I take a tumble trying to avoid a fallen tree. Blood seeps weakly from a scrape down my shin, so red it practically glows against this backdrop of the autumn woods. I look around me; from deep blacks through to browns, light tans to bright, vibrant greens, yellows, ochres, siennas, the pale blues of the sky. Nothing even close to the red of this blood. Look, I've made a contribution to nature's kaleidoscope! I set off again, wary at first, my adrenalin ebbing, picking up speed along the dry trail, the river on my right – and there, lying on the trail, one, two, three, tens, hundreds of leaves, suddenly, red as fire engines, discarded by a single tree. Red to challenge my blood-red. As if to say, anything you can do we can do better. I collect a few leaves to show my daughter, unsure if she'll think I'm weird (she's at an age when 'weird' is the peer group adjective of choice) or will happily fix the leaves to her windows or schoolbooks.

Bleeding is acceptable, of course. Scratches, scrapes, grazes, and even (to mountain runners in particular) gashes and tears – the blood-rite of passage. Drawing blood is a confirmation of your mortality, and a warning. I find it wise to listen. I picture myself ten years or so ago, clinging to rocks at Nan Bield Pass, a short arc of crags at the head of the Kentmere Horseshoe in the Lake District. It was snowing and the gale was throwing pellets of ice head-on against the high-level pass, straight into my face. The weather had been getting steadily more frightening for the last twenty minutes of my climb, the run up there becoming a painful slog through deepening snowdrifts and minimal visibility. The wind roared and barked, the view in front of me dropping to nothing more than a dense grey shroud. At Nan Bield, halfway around Kentmere's natural 'round', I knew that if I dropped off due south there was a path that would take me steadily, safely down to the valley below. I took it. As I dropped below the clouds, I looked back at the huge, darkening, booming swell I'd left behind. While there's much to celebrate in fearlessness, I'm always happy when fear plays its role as a safety valve; a self-made barrier against stupidity.

Extreme sports – when describing more than just a cool brand name used to sell prohibitively priced ski jackets and wraparound sunglasses – takes as one of its defining factors, along with the lure of the counter-culture (how come counter-culture always ends up being so damned expensive?) a high level of inherent danger. It's this flirting with injury (and possible death) that makes it so obviously appealing to so many people, and the very same flirting that makes it so unappealing to me. Despite my unnerving ability and desire to throw myself down scree slopes and clamber through unmarked forest trails, I have little ambition to put myself in real danger; I don't find it thrilling in the least. All the bloody knees, gashes and bruises collected over umpteen years of wild running serve as both trophies of having pushed myself to the edge of my ability (if only, at times, the ability to stay upright) and as reminders and warnings. See, you lost concentration and tore a small strip right down your shin – stop, stretch and look around. Soak up the adrenalin, and set off again.

17

There's a well-documented history of walking. A history peopled with poets, philosophers, scientists and educators; drug fiends, inventors, authors and *flâneurs*, flamboyant French libertarians in search of a world discovered by randomly wandering. Walking is celebrated, revered, assured its place in our culture and our past; despite the onslaught of the motor vehicle, walking is acknowledged as the ultimate metaphor for our journeying through life.

Charles Darwin famously had a 'Thinking Path' beyond the gardens of his house, a sand-covered trail through woods and along hedgerows. He would walk the path five times daily, citing it as an essential part of his problem-solving. Writers like Wordsworth, Thoreau and Baudelaire wrote passionately about walking, deeming it essential to our understanding of ourselves and our world. Wordsworth asked:

> Who doth not love to follow with his eye
> The windings of a public way? the sight,
> Familiar object as it is, hath wrought
> On my imagination since the morn
> Of childhood, when a disappearing line,
> One daily present to my eyes, that crossed

> *The naked summit of a far-off hill*
> *Beyond the limits that my feet had trod,*
> *Was like an invitation into space*
> *Boundless, or guide into eternity.*

Indeed, the literary world as we know it – mapped and populated – is a world of treks and walks, epic adventures scrawled in journals with frostbitten or bloodstained hands, *invitations into space*. Everyone understands a walk. American pioneers walking behind their covered wagons, the Long March of the communist Red Army, Hannibal and his elephants trekking over the Alps, England's unemployed Jarrow Marchers, the civil rights movement's Long Walk to Freedom. When, in 1965, Alexei Leonov exited the airlock of his Russian spacecraft and spent ten minutes floating several feet from the orbiting craft, he became the first man to walk in space, prompting the question: when is a walk not a walk? When, frankly, the word 'float' conjures up something altogether pleasant and relaxed, as opposed to adventurous and epic. That's why it was a space *walk*, not a space *float*.

Running doesn't have the same historical cachet. It has its stories and its histories, its tales and legends, but many of these concern not the adventuring lore of the walk but the desperation and necessity of running away, from the Great War's shell-shocked army deserters to the Deep South's runaway slaves, from the East Berliners who risked death to run across the no-man's-land of the Berlin Wall to South Vietnamese 9-year-old Kim Phúc, photographed running from the effects of burning napalm.

Always running away. Where are the stories of running towards? American writers retell clichéd stories of brave soldiers during the wars against the Native American; pursued by painted braves brandishing tomahawks, these young lads carried vital messages between regiments of embattled, outnumbered armies. Dashing through uncharted forests and leaping raging rivers, they left the Indian runners gasping for breath, staring in bewilderment as the keen and patriotic athletes gave them the slip (pant, pant, pant). And that's how the West was won, not with massacres and lies and betrayals but with handsome, sure-footed cross-country runners.

Much of running's sparsely written history begins with tales from ad-hoc and localized racing, not from organized track racing; village traditions involving all the adult menfolk, often naked, racing to a hilltop beacon and back again, for the prize of a slaughtered pig. Or long-distance runners in Victorian times racing 'fifty furlongs and five' over unploughed fields against leather-booted toffs on horseback. There is, of course, a rich history of necessary and imperative long-distance cross-country running, as recorded everywhere from painted cave walls to Greek vases; from hunting on foot to epic runs made by messengers to deliver news; and to the continuing tradition of running in Africa (where even today children can run long distances for food, water and education. A South African proverb says: 'Not everyone who chased the zebra caught it, but he who caught it, chased it.') There's relatively little of this history written down. The real embroidery of derring-do started in earnest when modern Olympians began swaying and stumbling around a measured cinder track, fatigued from exhaustion but able to breast the tape before the rest (in the Boy's Own tradition of stories, it

94

always helped when 'the rest' happened to be German). Suddenly running became spectacle and performance, enclosed and theatrical.

Most important among these Olympian tales, for me and for many athletes with half an eye on the cultural impact of sport on the world, are the performances that shake the disinterested viewer into sitting up and taking notice of this 'glorified pastime'. In essence, my favourite Olympic stories are not really about the Olympics at all. Jesse Owens' performances in the 1936 Berlin Olympics, the black sprinter who not only refused to give Adolf Hitler the Nazi salute but had the speed and determination to win four gold medals, are a landmark in the historical and political power of sport, not only at the Olympics themselves but afterwards, at home in America. Owens, despite being snubbed by Hitler (the Führer commenting later that 'people whose antecedents had come from the jungle, and thus had stronger physiques, should be excluded from future games') was remarkably even-handed about the whole affair, commenting that, 'Hitler didn't snub me – it was President Roosevelt who snubbed me. The President didn't even send me a telegram.' Back in the segregated USA, at his homecoming welcome on New York's Fifth Avenue, Owens was forced to ride the servants' elevator at the Waldorf-Astoria Hotel to reach the reception being given in his honour; neither Roosevelt nor following president Harry S. Truman ever publicly acknowledged his successes.

Emil Zatopek was a Czech long-distance track runner with a lopsided, awkward running style – arms flailing, head rolling grimly, comically, from side to side, mouth wide open and breathing heavily – who won four Olympic golds and set countless world records. Famous for his eccentricity in both style and method, the 'Czech Locomotive' became an unlikely victim of the lopsided, awkward world in which he belonged. An ardent communist, he held an important position for many years as a national hero, until 1968. During the eight-month-long Prague Spring, Zatopek openly supported the Czech government's attempts at liberalization and reform, opposing the eventual invasion by Russian tanks that crushed leader Alexander Dubček's attempted loosening of restrictions on the media, speech and travel. In return for this defiance, Zatopek was immediately expelled from the Communist Party and was forced to work in a uranium mine for six years for 'political rehabilitation'. Despite this, he faced post-running life with a stoic humour. Of his legendary and famously gruesome mid-race grimace, he remarked: 'I was not talented enough to run and smile at the same time.'

Zatopek's character is best seen in one act of human generosity that occurred well after he'd retired from competitive running. In 1968, the year of the Prague Spring, he was visited by the great Australian long-distance runner Ron Clarke, a man who respected and revered the older man's achievements. Clarke, despite being the 10,000-metres record holder, had never won an Olympic gold medal. On taking his leave, the pair shook hands warmly and Zatopek handed Clarke a small package which he didn't open until he'd boarded his home-bound plane. Inside the parcel was Emil's 10,000-metres Olympic gold medal and a note saying simply: 'Because you deserve it'. Zatopek and Owens didn't embody just athletic

96

excellence – their lives told a story about the world they lived in.

This is where running, and the culture of running, is at its best: when it speaks of the world in which it belongs. When we see not just the striding figure but the universe through which it runs. As a cultured and educated man, Zatopek was able to see his running as something more than winning and losing – running, even at its highest level, can still be that 'something more', especially if it can maintain its historical bond with the ground beneath us, by physically connecting us to that ground, step by step. Wild running, of course, makes this easier. As adventurer and writer John Muir discovered, it's difficult to ignore the damage being done to the environment when you have a personal stake in its survival.

18

John Muir, born in Scotland in 1838, famously came to embody a spirit of empathy and understanding with nature; but, more than that, he made wild adventuring *fun*. Having moved to Wisconsin as a botany student (though he never graduated; he was too eager to be out in the field, exploring) he discovered the art of just going out and wondering at the wild world. His incessant wanderings were notable in that he wrote about them, beautifully; he was able to put down on paper the passion and feeling he had for what he respect-fully capitalized as Nature. In September 1867, Muir embarked on a walk of 1,000 miles from Indiana to Florida, a journey he narrated in his book *A Thousand-Mile Walk to the Gulf*. He had no specific route, except to go by the 'wild-est, leafiest, and least trodden way I could find'. Companions talk of him 'whooping and howling at the vistas'. Even as he wrote daily of his travels and his delight in the natural world around him, he himself was continually reading the work of Ralph Waldo Emerson:

I see the spectacle of morning from the hill-top over against my house, from day-break to sun-rise, with emotions which an angel might share. The long slender bars of cloud float like fishes in the sea of crimson light. From the earth, as a shore, I look out into that silent sea. I seem to partake its rapid transformations: the active enchantment reaches my dust, and I dilate and conspire with the morning wind. How does Nature deify us with a few and cheap elements! Give me health and a day, and I will make the pomp of emperors ridiculous. (Emerson, from *Nature*, 1836)

People who love words, who love the world of words, understand the desire to discover (and rediscover) the places we'd forgotten about – not as picturesque views seen through car windows or photographs on wall calendars but as a moving, growing encyclopaedia under our feet. Our vocabulary is so much bigger when we step off the road. Look at the colours we have named in reference to Nature – fuchsia, aquamarine, almond, lavender, rose pink, chestnut, cornflower blue, moss green (I could go on). A huge and shifting palette; every day it changes, tints and hues responding to the diluting of the rain and the bleaching of the sun. The floor beneath our feet has its own lexicon, stretching away from asphalt and onto bedrock, crag, dust, earth, field, gravel, and through the alphabet of all that slippery, rutted, tangled stuff. The naming of the land reads like its own poem – doesn't *scree* sound like something to skid down, something loose and jagged? Writers like Muir and Emerson, Thoreau, Wordsworth and Whitman, they left the roads and a world opened up. And, in turn, their words read to us as an invitation to join them, to discover that new, vast ABC.

In this American adventure of a year, it's fast approaching winter and I'm still finding new and interesting trails and paths, mainly along the Brandywine Creek valley, three miles west of where we're living. Just this side of the Pennsylvania border and right where Wilmington – the largest city in Delaware, and at around 70,000 the same population as Burnley – comes to a sudden full stop, as if scared to cross the river. I run along both sides of the river's heavily wooded gorge, along and around the warren of unmarked trails and down to the bridge at Rockland. At the old stone crossing is Rockland Paper Mill, one of three defunct paper mills that were once powered by the Brandywine. Founded and built by a Scottish émigré, William Young, the mill produced several types of paper, originally using old linen and rags collected from local villagers' discarded sheets and clothing. By the late 1800s the mill was using what were said to be the widest paper machines in the world, producing magazine paper and paper for schoolbooks. The river, generally shallow and wide, flows narrow and fast here, funnelled towards the mill's waterwheels. Fish jump incessantly, the banks of the creek edging gradually down from the woods as sandbanks, and there's an old stone weir that you can cross on foot (if you enjoy getting wet). The mill closed in 1971 and was converted into upmarket housing (Spectacular One-Level Living! Offered at $625,000!), now peaceful and well kept. Crossing the river here, on this rambling paper trail of ideas and thoughts and good running routes, I can't help but sense the easy connection between the flow of the creek, the historical roll of the paper machines feeding hungrily on rags and wood pulp, the words written by adventurers in charcoal and graphite and the printed schoolbook texts of Wordsworth and Thoreau. I picture Muir and the rest,

100

out on the trails carrying their notepads and pencils, barely able to stop to take notes, such is their excitement and urgency to keep moving.

Walkers and ramblers often talk disparagingly of trail runners, muttering something to the effect that slowing down might give us more time to appreciate our surroundings. To the hill and country walker who wonders if the runner is going too fast to see anything – of course not, we watch every step, look out for every possible up and down, twist and turn. Our footing and our precious bones depend on us looking ahead, looking around, watching the weather, the trees, each dip and jut in the ground. In Britain I'm often spoiled for views on mountain runs – the hills are usually treeless and, if the cloud allows, every few hundred yards affords a different view. Here on America's East Coast the hills and valleys are generally forested, deep dark acres of tree trunks flanking every trail. During September's Conestoga Trail Race in Pennsylvania's Lancaster County, the steep wooded hillsides suddenly give way to House Rock Overlook, a rocky outcrop clear of the trees that looks down and across the Susquehanna River. The vast and panoramic view, coupled with the miles of twisting, turning forest and creek trail covered in relative darkness, makes the astonishing vista all the more breathtaking. (Breathtaking isn't something you particularly wish for during a race, especially after a long, steep climb.) After several miles along a zigzagging barely marked trail worming its way up and down through the forest, the suddenness of the view is a shock: hundreds of feet down to the broad, fast-flowing river, dotted with islands, its far shore rising spectacularly in a mirror image of the thickly wooded valley side we've just clambered up. After so many miles of rationed sunlight and silhouetted tree trunks, the open burst of sky, land and river leaves me blinking and squinting against the sun, straining to drink it all in before tumbling back into the forest.

I'm always surprised by runners who can carry on, heads down, through such views. Here's a moment to savour; the mind's quick snapshot, labelled and filed. A reward to carry around long after the bruised ankles and tired limbs have forgotten the race. As I reach this spectacular view I instinctively turn to the runner just behind me and exclaim, 'look at that . . . just look at that!' and he grins, looks and nods. We stop to gaze for a few seconds, taking it in, before setting off again. Frankly, I've never run so fast that I can't see the world around me, the world under my studded shoes.

Reading John Muir's travelogues, diaries and essays, one thing that keeps jumping from the pages along with his enthusiasm and zest is how much he runs. Not only runs, but leaps, slides, scoots, hops and races, up and down the mountain trails, across rivers and through forests. He hears a storm outside his cabin in the heart of Yosemite and runs out, deep into the woods, selects a tall, sturdy tree and climbs high into its swaying branches to watch the spectacle. During mid-winter, hearing the first rumblings of an avalanche from the peaks above him, he leaps onto the oncoming snowfall, surfing it for half a mile until it deposits him gently at the foot of the mountain. It's almost as if his sense of joy propels him forward, urging him to break into a run whenever he can, notebook and pencils tucked into his shirt and a pair of leather-soled boots to complement his thick grey suit. Life in the places he visits is too full to take at a slow pace:

> *If for a moment you are inclined to regard these taluses* [heaps of rock fragments at the foot of the cliffs] *as mere draggled, chaotic dumps – climb to the top of one of them, and run down without any haggling, puttering hesitation, boldly jumping from boulder to boulder with even speed. You will then find your feet playing a tune, and quickly discover the music and poetry of these magnificent rock piles – a fine lesson; and all Nature's wildness tells the same story – the shocks and outbursts of earthquakes, volcanoes, geysers, roaring, thundering waves and floods, the silent uprush of sap in plants, storms of every sort – each and all are the orderly beauty-making love-beats of Nature's heart.*
> (Yosemite, March 1872)

Muir's enthusiasm was shared by literary contemporaries – both in America and in Britain – who were discovering for themselves the importance of nature, and the desire to travel through it without desiring to dig below it, build on it or stake a claim to it. Not that everyone shared this first bloom of enlightened thinking about the land. By the nineteenth century there were long-distance foot-races being organized across America and Europe, with winners standing to earn good money. Notable contestants advertised themselves with displays of showmanship and an air of carnival, competing against horses and around dog-racing tracks, and as these races became more popular they inevitably attracted huge-scale betting along with attendant accusations of bribery, fraud and cheating. It wasn't long before plans were being made to stage a modern marathon race strictly for amateurs, in Greece as part of the first Olympic Games. This first revival of the marathon – held over twenty-five miles between Marathon and Athens in 1896 – featured amateur runners from several countries, fortified at the start with milk and beer. Along the route they were given wine and cognac and were accompanied by cheering crowds, cyclists and all the fun of the fair. A local Greek man named Louis Spiridon won the race and was offered jewellery, several proposals of marriage and a lifetime's free shave at a barber's shop along with a year's supply of chocolate; despite the cloak of amateurism, the festive atmosphere of the street fair persisted. John Muir, of course, would have scoffed at this carny-style jollification of running, if only for its insistence upon sticking to the roads – in another diary entry from 1872, he admonishes himself for having spent too long in the city, away from his beloved Yosemite, 'terribly dazed and confused with the dust and din'. Suffering a heavy fall somewhere above Mirror Lake, he addressed himself: 'That is what you get by intercourse with stupid town stairs, and dead pavements.'

The modern Olympic Games were always part of a much broader context than simply athleticism; from the beginning, they were used as diplomatic gatherings and political showcases. The Olympic myth – that the Games were a way of encouraging the suspension of hostilities between warring nations – hid a background of political and armed intervention. Despite the success of the first Games in 1896, they were marred by animosity between Pierre de Coubertin (founder of the Olympics) and the

Greek royal family. At both this and at least the two subsequent Olympics, leading runners in the marathon race were accused, exposed or disqualified for hitching rides in vehicles and taking short cuts. Louis Spiridon never ran again, instead leading a quiet life as a farmer; his last public appearance was as a guest at the 1936 Berlin Olympics, where he presented a symbolic olive branch to Hitler. Five years later, Germany invaded Greece.

John Muir died in 1914, leaving as a legacy the Sierra Club, the oldest and largest grassroots environmental organization in the United States. Its motto, more or less unchanged since then, is *Explore, enjoy and protect the planet.* John Muir was, as we can discover in his writings, a man who *enjoyed* the planet. In his accounts of explorations, he topples and falls, slides and stumbles, all with a sense of delight. His articles and essays, compiled from a scribbled notebook he carried with him on his adventures, practically jump from the paper, leaping from paragraph to paragraph before scaling around the jutting crag face of a turning page. (All the more ironic, then, that in the local Barnes & Noble bookstore his books are listed as being in the 'Homes & Gardens' section.) Muir lived minute to minute, and seldom had a long-term plan; and as with most wild running, the finishing wasn't the purpose; the purpose was in simply being there.

'I only went out for a walk, and finally concluded to stay out till sundown, for going out, I found, was really going in.' (John Muir)

Often when I race I pay little attention to the finishing results, sitting there with my crumpled cup of water, exhausted and elated in equal measures. I replay the race in my head, picturing corners and descents and falls, like watching a good film twice. When I was younger, when I first started to run well in hill races, I used to wonder if my love of trail running was dependent upon success, on winning categories or finishing in front of rivals from other clubs. But I got older, and my results started to drop away, and I realize now as I slip down through the field that no, my love of the sport doesn't depend upon some measure of success – all I demand of myself is the necessary fitness to enjoy running and racing. If that means walking up a steep ascent as others run past me, then so be it. It's fun. It always has been, and will remain so, until my body decides it can't do it any more.

Here's a joke I found on the internet: 'Last year I entered the New York City Marathon. I was right at the back. The slowest of the slow. It was embarrassing. And the guy who was in front of me, second to last, was making fun of me. He said, "Hey buddy, how does it feel to be last?" I replied: "Do you want to know?" and I dropped out.' (From Runtheplanet.com)

19

My dad was a fell runner for many years, and stopped running competitively only when cancer almost killed him and rubbished his immune system into the bargain. He wasn't a great fell racer, but he loved it. Prided himself on not finishing last, but would occasionally finish second to last. That was enough of a victory for him. Then he'd sit and tell you his experience of the course, every crag hop and scramble, mud splash and tumble. He doesn't race any more but still jogs and walks on the hills, tentatively and at an easy pace. He can't stop. He thought the cancer, once it had been declared as remissive, might reduce him to a life of gentle strolling. But there he is, still pad-pad-padding up the slopes of Pen-Y-Ghent to watch the annual Three Peaks hill race.

'How does it feel to be near the back of a race?'

'Well, the views are just as good, and you get to spend longer out there amongst the landscape.'

Wild racing, as opposed to wild running (though the two are not necessarily opposed) is a strange and complex thing. Although I run most days, I relish the races. The occasional grit-your-teeth competition, the eyeballs-out desperation to push harder than the runner in front of you, adds a different complexion to the simple joy of running. It doesn't stop me luxuriating in that natural bombardment of the senses that is slithering around on a storm-soaked trail high on a moor; if anything, it heightens the amount of attention I have to pay to the world moving under my feet. Races give me impetus to run regularly – you can enjoy running without much training, but it's less easy to enjoy racing on very little background running. And races give me an excuse to discover new places. Especially in America, where everywhere is new to me – where a race venue can open up a Pandora's Box of trails, hills and paths. Races give me focus, something to aim for, something to look forward to. Races give me the discipline not to spend every weekend travelling to concerts, drinking and staying up late. Races remind me how to stick at something, how to get to the end of a thing without shrugging my shoulders and dropping out. Races make me happy. Races make me nervous, excited, ecstatic. Through racing I've been to places I never would have heard of, places I've since returned to again and again. Races have their own history and their own character; they uphold tradition, put me right there in the photograph with Ernest Dalzell, 1910, winning the Burnsall Show Fell Race in a record time. Races are communal, the competitive urge staying close to the camaraderie of a shared experience. In off-road racing, this is always the case – as if even the winners, the super-athletes who pour all the weekly, monthly, yearly hours and effort into competing at the top level of the sport, understand that the trail itself – the mountain, the forest, the rain, the tumbling earth – is bigger than all of us.

But despite all this, it's not racing that *defines* wild

running. Making a concerted effort to leave the tarmac is personal; it's an escape from the congregation. Why make the leap from the overpopulated world of the road race in order to join another, albeit more pleasant, game of follow-my-leader? Some of the popular mountain races can attract many hundreds of runners, and it's difficult to link a seemingly never-ending ribbon of mucky vests and shorts worming its way along a skyline with wild running's promise of space, freedom and escape.

But this is, after all, an eclectic jumble of a sport. It is, in effect, as private or as communal as you want it to be. Some fear that a rise in the number of people taking to the hills, trails and forests will do untold damage to the sport; in this, they almost exclusively refer to racing rather than running. There's a big difference. Much as I love racing, it's the running – the muddy morning slogs into the hills and mountains – that dominates, not the racing. If a race is too big for its studded boots, then don't do it. While there are continuing battles over access, environmental damage and overerosion, better to find the races that enjoy small entry lists, minimal organization and the sense of freedom from the crowd. I'm not here to warn and finger-wag; the sport (like the vast areas of virtually unpopulated wild earth around us) is big enough for us. I'm not here to turn you away, I'm here to invite you in . . .

Listen to me, sounding like a street preacher. Thumping my copy of Bill Smith's *Studmarks on the Summits* against a fold-out pulpit set up on some particularly busy city junction, shouting over the blare of the traffic. Some people stop and watch because I'm the amiable nutter, free entertainment, the revivalist tubthumper (!) on a mission from the Church of Pastoral Scrambling. And lo he told them, flee, flit, fly! Leave the road of sin and follow the one true path – that one, heading straight up the mountain!

As a boy I would accompany Elders from the Mormon Church – our family were all converts – on a weekly mission to help reconnect with those followers who had fallen (or jumped!) by the wayside. We'd go out on a Wednesday evening, calling on unsuspecting ex-Mormons, seeing the barely masked antipathy in their faces as they opened the door to find us standing there, Bibles under our arms. I used to dread those Wednesdays. I disliked the idea of pestering people who'd made their decision to leave – I grew to feel that the truly faithful wouldn't need this kind of prodding. Often we'd stand there, my older partner trying to convince someone to let us in for a few minutes, to chat, to say a prayer. *How's little Elizabeth? Really? Oh lovely. And Ronnie, still doing the football practice? Lovely to see you again. Can I leave a few leaflets? As I say, it'd be lovely to see you and Katherine and the kids down at the Chapel.* And all the while I could hear the football on the TV, knowing we were never going to get in and that next time we called they'd have a spyhole in the door and we'd hear the shuffling but the door wouldn't open, at least not while Liverpool v. Newcastle was on the telly.

The need to proselytize – to recruit and convert – runs deep within Christianity. It derives almost entirely from one directive, given by Jesus, at the end of the Gospel of Matthew: 'Go ye therefore, and teach all nations, baptizing them in the name of the Father, and of the Son, and of the Holy Ghost: Teaching them to observe all things whatsoever I have commanded you.'

It's what Christians call 'the Great Commission of Jesus', the edict and order to go further than simply enjoying and indulging your personal belief – no, you must teach others to do the same as you. Now if only Jesus had said, 'Go ye therefore, and luxuriate in your faithfulness. Worship, pray, take the sacrament, wear a habit or a wimple if you must. And if other people – non-believers – see that you are happy and amiable, maybe they'll want to join you in that worship. And if they don't, then fine, let them go to hell in a handcart, as long as they're happy. But don't bug them about it.' See, no strapping explosives around your waist and walking into Holy Temples. No Crusades (past and present). No destruction of indigenous peoples' lands and customs in the name of God and Allah. No knocking on doors on Wednesday evenings in Burnley, wishing I was hanging out on street corners and chatting to girls.

When I first began to discover runnable paths and trails, when I first ran up a mountain (and ran back down again), when I first raced around the Yorkshire fells – I knew I'd found something life-changing. A mud-splattered baptism in the storm-swelled quagmire of Pudsey Beck, a forest-track-to-Damascus moment along the canal from my house in Leeds to Bramley Falls woods, with its dirt paths snaking through the trees, abandoned buildings and open fields like the electrical wiring in an old house, ancient and underused. I was in heaven (Oh Lord, now he really is the city-centre nutter). To be fair, it's taken me almost twenty-five years to write this book, since that marathon in Bolton in 1981, where I'd decided simply that once was enough and left it at that. But here I am, preacher and propagandist, spreading the Good News and damning with fire and brimstone those who dare spend their Sundays pounding the roads and looking at their split mile times.

I can't help myself. I'm a born-again wild runner, and, friends, I need to tell you about it. Heeeaaa! How can I begrudge the Mormon spirit of door-knocking? You can always say no. Like the pioneering poet-wanderers, I feel the urge to tell people what a world there is to be found, *out there*. Out there beyond the shade of skyscrapers, out of range of the right-angle corners, a world without the chimera of a perfectly flat 26.2 miles. I can't tell you what you'll find, of course – it'll be your discovery, not mine. I don't claim any expertise in being 'out there'. I can't name the birdsong, don't know the difference between a Boxelder and a Paperbark Maple and, other than in my running shoes, can't tie a good knot (clove hitch? Bowline? Reef?). The seductiveness of discovery! Brothers and sisters, mine eyes have seen the glory of . . . etc.

20

Obesity, the main, preventable cause of death, is threatening to turn us into a world that literally eats itself to extinction. Some say that long before the oil runs out we'll see the ballooning pandemic of ill health threaten to turn entire nations into wheezing, immobile lumps. In a league table of countries with the highest levels of clinical obesity, Britain is third and America is first (See the big foam hands in the air. 'Number One! Number One!'). In these two countries, today's children – according to a *New England Journal of Medicine* report – are likely to have shorter, less healthy lives than their parents. Obesity in children has tripled since 1980. It continues to grow.

Me and my older sister, she eight years old and me seven in our matching duffel coats, were in Burnley town centre with my mum, each of us clutching one of her hands, bored and tired. Traipsing round the shops and supermarkets, carrying bags and looking for puddles to jump in. It was a Saturday and this was the weekly routine, loading up with carrier bags full of tins and potatoes, being treated to black pudding in the market hall (plenty of vinegar, please) before waiting in a queue for the bus outside the Empire Bingo Hall on St James' Street. Only today was different. We were going to the Safeway near the bus station, the Safeway with its huge aisles and chequered linoleum floor, and, best of all, with its automatic doors. No, really. You just stood in front of them – on the rubber mat – and the door swung open, smooth and inviting, chrome and glass, shhhwooooshhh. My mum had to cajole and beg us to stop returning to the doors to watch them opening and shutting – we tried to see how lightly we could step on the mat, to see how close we could get, trying to make the doors open with fingertips, lips and hips. Yes, there were rockets sending men into space (to *spacewalk*) and, yes, there were turbojet-powered cars capable of speeds of almost 600 mph. But they were on TV and in the newspapers, not in Burnley town centre on a Saturday morning in the rain. A door that opened automatically. Shhhwooooshhh. Imagine.

As we grew older, occasional trips to Manchester (the closest big city, twenty-five miles south and an hour on the double-decker bus) meant not only the modern world of automatic doors but the added delight of department store escalators. Debenhams had a whole series of escalators that took us up five floors to the haberdashery department – such an exotic name for the button and zip floor – and, fuelled by tales of children getting trapped in the top and bottom of the claw-edged moving stairway, we ritualized every jump both onto and off the escalator into an Olympic sport. Stairs that moved. Whatever next.

Then there was the TV remote control, which was a shoebox-sized module attached to the TV by an extending curly wire. When we first had a TV that had just such a remote, the whole family was gobsmacked by the apparent need to have buttons on a hand-held box. Look, the

TV is only three feet away! Who wouldn't be able to get out of their armchair to switch channels (there were only three channels, after all)? Of course, within a week we were fighting for stewardship of the remote and, when we forgot to rescue it from the set top, we begrudged having to heave ourselves three feet from the settee to retrieve it.

It's the way of the world, of course. According to Dr Diane Finegood, director of the nutrition, metabolism and diabetes unit of the Canadian Institutes of Health Research, 'A drop in obesity will come when stairs are placed more prominently than escalators [and] when we build our environments in a way that people can actually walk to their destinations.' That's the shorthand version. Basically our obesity levels are an inherent part of the world we're creating – an automated world. We communicate without sharpening pencils or hunting for envelopes, without licking stamps or walking to the postbox. I'm writing this without having to reach out and swoosh a typewriter's paper carriage (ding!) at the end of every line or scurry around in a desk drawer looking for the Tipp-Ex. It's so often assumed that the increase in everything from heart disease, diabetes, colon cancer, osteoporosis and obesity can be put down to overeating, or at least eating the wrong kinds of food. Dieticians, doctors and data refute this: statistics show that the main and overriding cause of obesity is inactivity.

In 2005 *The Lancet* carried a report that stated that '. . . findings so far indicate that the drastic decline in habitual activity during adolescence might be a major factor in the doubling of the rate of obesity development in the USA in the past two decades, since no concomitant increase in energy intake was apparent'.

Only around 10 per cent of marathon runners are under the age of thirty, a fact that suggests to me (without tying myself in statistical knots) that marathons just aren't appealing to young people. According to a survey by the US National Sporting Goods Association in 2003, the most favoured participant sports outside school for twelve- to seventeen-year-olds were, in order of popularity, basketball, bicycle riding, inline skating, fishing, baseball, golf, skateboarding and snowboarding. I'd hazard a guess that kids have no desire to emulate their mums and dads pulling agonized faces at marathon finish lines, checking their expensive watches before collapsing. You've spent your adolescence watching them heading out on their daily training runs ready to race their demons in a shirt declaring 'The Work Doesn't Start Until the Pain Kicks In', and you know it's the last thing you want to do. 'Look, son, watch me run in straight lines for twenty-six miles on the hard concrete pavement. One day all this could be yours.'

Dr Lisa Sutherland of the University of North Carolina explains the problem in one rapid-fire burst of statistics: 'From 1980 through 2000, obesity increased 10 percent, physical activity decreased 13 percent and caloric intake rose 1 percent among U.S. adolescents.'

If we're to challenge the all-conquering fatness regime that is the video game then we need a better weapon than marathon running. It may help with a mid-life crisis but it's no answer to the Xbox, the PlayStation, the DS and the Wii. The gym is no better an enticement for kids – what twelve-year-old wants to spend an hour in a sweat-stinking room full of adults and jogging machines? Howard Chudacoff, a cultural historian at Brown

University, in Providence, Rhode Island, notes that for most of human history what children did when they played was roam in packs large or small, more or less unsupervised, and engage in freewheeling, imaginative play. They were pirates and princesses, aristocrats and action heroes. They improvised play, on street corners or in backyards, and, says Chudacoff, this play was self-regulated, unruled and unruly.

This all changed as the focus for 'play' began to be seen as objects, as toys – spurred on by aggressive advertising by toy manufacturers. Coupled with a greatly increased element of parental fear (when the bogeyman of our imaginations was sold back to us as the paedophile, the abuser, the child kidnapper), play began to become regulated, pre-packaged, with pre-existing rules. As a young boy I remember street games based roughly on hide-and-seek, tag or knock-and-run turning into mass-participation, sprawling games that went on for hours, spread out across local streets and playgrounds. Expeditions to the nearest bit of countryside became day-long adventures full of cuts, bruises, discoveries and dares; bicycle rides were often ill-prepared jaunts that, along the way, became epics.

What children have lost, according to Chudacoff, is the ability to learn about regulating themselves. In much of modern running, we see a world of delineated routes and distances, where the running store provides our clothing, footwear, gels and watches, where we follow a blue line painted on the road, and where electronic measurement and a big clock on top of a car allows us to accurately (to $1/_{1000\text{th}}$ of a second) judge our time against other marathon runners the world over.

Let's just assume for the sake of sepia-tinted, Vaseline-lens nostalgia that children were encouraged to rediscover the joy of running through open country, along trails, crossing rivers and climbing fallen trees. Wouldn't that open-ended, improvised sense of play be more attractive than the grey and black city-street plod-plod-plod of marathon running? In northern England on occasional Saturday afternoons I watch kids as young as seven or eight doing organized children's fell races, charging up and down hills and slipping around in the mud, out of breath but loving being wild, outside in the wide-open space. And these kids aren't the same as some of the kids I see at my daughter's school, slow and heavy. Look at children when they play video games – look at their eyes. Controlled, corralled, tamed. See them in the woods, balancing on rocks and clambering up riverbanks, their eyes free and fierce.

21

It's winter, and there's a blizzard coming in. Sweeping across America, dumping up to twenty inches of snow and ice as it blows through; TV news reporters in bright nylon and expensive wool face camera as cars dance on the roads behind them. They love it – it's drama, and as close as you get to real disaster or war without fearing for your life. I'm in Concord, Massachusetts, a tiny old colonial town outside Boston, a town of museums and gift shops. Every building is panelled in white wood, clean and neat, but right now they're all disappearing beneath a dense grey and white haze of heavy afternoon snow. Shops are closing, and people shuffle to cars, escaping early.

Just as the storm begins to switch from flurry to bluster (that's somewhere between blast and blizzard) I pull on a balaclava, thick gloves and studded shoes and head off to find the place where Henry David Thoreau lived in 1845 in a tiny wooden shack on the shore of a small lake called Walden Pond. It was here that he wrote his seminal back-to-nature rallying cry, *Walden*, here where, for a while, he stripped his life of the nation's growing consumerism and replaced it with an adventurous self-sufficiency.

At Walden, a short, icy run away from the nearby town of Concord, there's no one. Forests can be spectacularly lonely and isolating places, no more so than in the dead of winter, at the head of a storm, the birds and deer and foxes huddled somewhere, silent. Is there anywhere more enchanting than thick forest in the snow? My parents used to have a mounted reproduction of Pieter Brueghel's *Hunters in the Snow* on the living room wall; it was part of the furniture. It survived for two decades or more – the seventies and eighties – outliving the stereogram, the turquoise trimphone, the automatic potato peeler (automatic in the sense that it had a hand-crank) and at least two three-piece suites.

I knew *Hunters in the Snow* like the back of my hand. Every square inch of it – the old woman carrying firewood, the skaters on the frozen lake, three children chasing each other across the ice; the church in the distance, frozen rivers zigzagging off towards the mountains. I loved to point out the place where the old woman by the fire suddenly faded away into the doorway behind her, the artist somehow forgetting to paint in the rest of her. And everywhere, snow, deep snow, for the hunters to trudge through, to weigh down the rooftops of the cottages, to cover the frozen wheel of the watermill, to smother the fields and paths. I loved it because it wasn't Disney snow, it wasn't sound-tracked by sleighbells and decorated with vivid greens and reds – this was cold, heavy and beautifully muted and muffled. That's the word – muffled. In this forest outside Concord, the wide-open pond stretching off to my left and the trees rising up the hill to my right, everything is muffled. The more it snows, the more muffled the landscape. Muffle: originally meaning to wrap up or enfold. That's what the snow is doing, wrapping up the landscape, until there's just my

120

breathing and the dull pad of my feet on the snow. I run to the original spot where Thoreau built his one-room house and stop. Absolute silence. Considering how close we are to Concord's bustling little main street, less than two miles to the north, the remoteness is shocking. Through the moving, falling curtain of snowflakes I can just about make out the tiny railway line that passed through the forest some way behind Thoreau's hut, a reminder for him of the quicker pace of life away from the Pond. I turn and run off around the perimeter of the iced-over lake, seeing no sign of the Pond's water, only a wide expanse of snow; without a map to tell me otherwise, this might as well be a flat, open plain. The running is difficult, with every step a sinking and pulling in the crunching drifts, ice forming on the balaclava covering my mouth. The trees creak and heave, fence posts become submerged and the only signs of animal life are occasional small birds, dashing for shelter.

It's not difficult to place yourself in such easy wildness. To get out of the town and immerse yourself in nature's playful unpredictability. Here at Walden Pond, skirting sensibly the right side of danger, a heavy blizzard is an opportunity to get to grips with all these words, these thoughts, about wild running. The forced conclusion of an hour spent crashing and wallowing along the Pond's edge is only that I want other people to do this, to try this. To see an approaching storm – rain, snow, wind – and briefly swap the comfortable huddle for the wet-feet, stinging-face blast of a run like this. As I reach the small road that leads back to Concord I can feel the storm continuing to build, the tracks and trails becoming impassable. I get my breath back for a minute and look back across the stark, blank and silent Pond, surrounded by its woods spreading eastwards towards Minute Man State Park, towards more forests and more ponds, trying to imagine life in a tiny cabin with a blazing fire, a pan of soup and a book full of words.

The American Revolutionary War began in this region (Emerson wrote in his 'Concord Hymn' of the 'shot heard 'round the world') with the Americans chasing the British out of the area and back to Boston, where they might get on the first boat back to Blighty and stop meddling in other countries' affairs. (Judging by the ruthless two hours of questioning I had to suffer at immigration in Philadelphia trying to enter the USA recently, I get the feeling some of the locals haven't quite forgotten we were once at war.) The area is awash with colonial paraphernalia, Stars and Stripes flags and monuments to heroic militia. Strange, then, that Concord shares its heritage with an unkempt and bearded pacifist who spent years in a wooden shack at the furthermost edge of polite Massachusetts society, excusing himself from the jumble-tumble of the town. Even as he lived, revelling in the quirks of his passionate disdain for fashion and custom, he was ignored by society at large. During his lifetime, *Walden* sold a measly 300 copies a year. He was unknown outside the immediate area; this was the home of the American Revolution, what business would anyone want with an itinerant poet-philosopher?

Retreating back to Concord from the woods of Thoreau's old homestead (and I have to be quick, before I get marooned by the blizzard . . .) it's easy to understand how and why he came to live and work there. It's only just beyond the town boundary – hardly 'wild' – but is effectively and utterly cut off from the everyday buzz of urban life. Inside his little hut were only a stove, a bed, three wooden chairs and a writing desk. The desk was placed directly under one of two small windows, from which the writer might watch the forest dressing and undressing itself through the changing seasons. In truth, reading Thoreau's odyssey of his time spent at Walden Pond, I get the idea he was a cranky and difficult man; his self-imposed isolation – his attempt at an obstinate and huffy asceticism (marginally more fun than sitting on top of a pole in the desert) is almost perverse. But the inverted snobbery of such exiled anti-consumerism is balanced by his exuberant joyousness and what John Burroughs calls 'certainly the most delicious piece of brag in literature'. Thoreau himself wrote of his time at Walden that 'I do not propose to write an ode to dejection, but to brag as lustily as Chanticleer in the morning, standing on his roost, if only to wake my neighbours up.' Brag – a word we connect with boastfulness and crowing, but which can just as well serve as the trumpeted yell of triumph.

As a writer and detailer of ideas, Thoreau is inspiring and insightful. It was he who noted that 'the great mass of mankind lead lives of quiet desperation'. You can't fault Thoreau for rigorously testing his theories personally – whatever his time at Walden might have been, it certainly wasn't quietly desperate. Thoreau's most telling gifts to the world were undoubtedly his radical and uncompromising ideas on our responsibilities as individuals – essentially, he was urging people to think for themselves. The world loves an iconoclast, a free-thinker (often with the benefit of hindsight) and Thoreau exemplifies that rebellious character; and it was while living on Walden Pond that he truly discovered a connection between being an agitator, a firebrand – an anti-slavery, anti-war pacifist – and being a part of the natural world around him. Yes, he railed against government and wrote of civil disobedience and conscientious objection; but at its source, this fire was fuelled by an uncompromised love of nature.

Snow is a beautiful leveller (literally). Even in our towns and cities it blankets and lays waste to carefully signposted road markings and boundary lines. During New York's winter snowstorm this year I went running from a friend's house in Brooklyn, marvelling at the blurring of the landscape. Street and pavement blended into park, and it seemed like everywhere was off-road, a dog walk, a play space. There was an outlaw mentality to car parking: where two days previously there'd been ruthless zoning and regulation, now there was abandonment and make-do. If you found a kerbside space, fill it. Most cars were buried and immobile anyway, double-parked, skew-whiff and splayed, happily disobedient.

When the snows came this winter, so did the ice; Delaware's Brandywine River, wide and shallow, stopped dead in its tracks. On long runs along its banks, as morning sun broke through the early sky's murk, the ice on the river began to slowly melt, creaking and squeaking and groaning. More than once I thought I heard a cry, looking across the river towards the far bank before realizing the ice was sighing as it twisted itself into the relative warmth of the day.

And in Concord village, the snow continues to fall,

smothering and muffling. Cars are infrequent and people talk of being snowed in for days. I picture 27-year-old Henry David Thoreau, in the winter of 1845, shoring up his tiny home and stoking up the wood-burning stove before sitting at his desk, looking out of the window at the snow-covered pond and picking up his pen. His friend Ellery Channing referred to Thoreau's cabin as 'a wooden inkstand'.

In the streets and in society I am almost invariably cheap and dissipated, my life is unspeakably mean. No amount of gold or respectability would in the least redeem it, dining with the Governor or a member of Congress! But alone in the distant woods or fields, in unpretending sprout-lands or pastures tracked by rabbits, even in a bleak and, to most, cheerless day, like this, when a villager would be thinking of his inn, I come to myself, I once more feel myself grandly related, and that cold and solitude are friends of mine . . . I thus dispose of the superfluous and see things as they are, grand and beautiful. I have told many that I walk every day about half the daylight, but I think they do not believe it. I wish to get the Concord, the Massachusetts, the America, out of my head and be sane a part of every day. (Henry David Thoreau)

And that, in a nutshell, is an opportunity we can all take – to be sane for a part of each day, to pull on a pair of running shoes and, in the 'unpretending sprout-lands', get to feeling grandly related.

22

Thoreau's depiction of life away from nature as 'cheap, dissipated and mean' could sound like either the generalized slur of a grouch or the straightforward frankness of a realist. It depends where you happen to be standing – I'm standing in the middle of a zoo, hands deep in pockets and scarf wrapped tight, on a Friday morning in a freezing New Jersey December, and it doesn't get much meaner than this.

I'm standing with my face up close to a wire enclosure, looking straight at an adult lion. Indolent, lethargic, sluggish. It lollops across the enclosure. It has around forty square feet of space, which it shares with another lion, smaller and even less inclined to move. Forty square feet is roughly a quarter of the space given over to the zoo's family cafeteria, with its pre-packed sandwiches and Soft-Whip ice cream. Next to the lions' patchy-scrub-ground enclosure, with only the wire fence between them, is the tigers' forty square feet. Same again, two tigers, idle and impassive. Animals from two separate continents, squashed (these animals would look squashed in an enclosure fifty times the size) and packaged and presented to us to gawp at. The ground is hard and practically bare.

And over here, boys and girls, the wolves' enclosure

next to the caged sheep. And the bears adjoining the young deer. All on the same scrubby earth, unsheltered and dirty. If these juxtapositions were designed to excite the animals into 'acting up' for our benefit, it doesn't work; they've all long since become accustomed to both their own and their neighbours' impotence. It's one of the saddest sights I've seen for a while, not primarily because I'm distressed by the utterly indecent conditions of the animals. I'm moved more by what it says about us, about a society we see as improving and evolving. This unkempt, ill-kept zoo should be a forgotten relic, but instead it just reminds me of how we're so easily giving up on the wildness that is part of us. The passion, the adventure, the lack of inhibition, the natural joy and excitement of play. See this lion, dull and boring, pathetic, even. It has the possibility, somewhere in its memory and genetics, of running up to 40 mph, of hunting and chasing, of mating with its partner up to forty times in a day.

Male lions live up to eight years longer in captivity than in the wild. Eight more years of scratching around, pacing, yawning, stretching and sleeping. Eight more years of being fed and watered on demand, of lying in the sun watching kids through a fence; kids who think you're boring for just lying there.

I read a comment recently suggesting that, instead of driving to the gym and spending an hour exercising on a jogging machine, people might think about running to the gym and playing car-driving video games for an hour. Spending an afternoon at this zoo reminds me of why I'm self-contracted to be a missionary for wild running, for refusing the inhibited, unnatural falseness of the city marathon. Because the marathon dislocates us from the earth we're running on. It separates us from the essential facts of our ancestry and the exquisite peace available to us in off-road running.

John Muir wrote: *'Thousands of tired, nerve-shaken, over-civilized people are beginning to find out that going to the mountain is going home; that wildness is necessity; that mountain parks and reservations are useful not only as fountains of timber and irrigating rivers, but as fountains of life.'*

Back in Arden, Delaware, as I step lightly from stone to stone in the river, avoiding the booby-trap green moss and the unstable boulders, my foot lands on a cold, grey, exposed bedrock just as a snake darts from it, winding and uncoiling into the river and away, gone, even as my foot has found balance. This pattern is repeated as I step-step-step, wherever in the countryside I run – animals flapping, dashing, sneaking and galloping away as I approach. They don't easily allow me to stare, take photographs of, or feed them. They know better. They know to run, and they know where to run.

23

On the corner of Manhattan's First Avenue and East 116 Street, halfway up the four-mile straight run towards the Bronx, the road is awash with Gatorade. It spreads, sweet and sticky, dotted and spotted with a thousand emptied paper cups, an alien landscape. The crowds are thinner here, the whooping less insistent. The runners – at around the sixteen-mile mark – are no longer acknowledging the crowd; I look for signs of smiles but can't find a single one. Every runner looks like they're in pain, sucking their emotions deep inside in an attempt to block out the aches and twinges and jolts and pulls. In the deadpan, utterly dejected words of Johnny Rotten – at the Sex Pistols' last ever concert in San Francisco – this looks like 'no fun. No fun at all.'

In the blocked-off roads at each side of the marathon route, in contrast, there's a sense of carnival and space, groups of boys throwing footballs high into the air and running between the parked cars. These streets are car-free only once each year – what a treat! Fire engines and cop cars sit at each intersection, police and fire-fighters sitting on car hoods and leaning against their doors, chewing toothpicks and staring into the strangely compelling caterpillar of slow-moving multicoloured suffering working its way up First Avenue. For the runners, this is about achievement and self-motivation, about endurance and above all about finishing. The bit in the middle – the twenty-four miles between the exhilaration of the first one and the relief of the last one – isn't supposed to be 'fun'.

A cop asks me to move my bicycle away from the road, despite it being behind barriers. He isn't being unpleasant, just doing what he's been told to do – keep the sidewalk clear, let New Yorkers see the runners, give people space to hold up their signs (even though, by this point, barely a runner raises a glance toward the spectators). Let's keep this whole thing moving, moving, moving.

A runner slows, stops and starts again. He begins to wander from barrier to barrier. A spectator shouts 'Follow the line! Follow the line!' The runner pours water from a paper cup over his head, shakes it, focuses on the blue line and sets off again. A long, slow shuffle, head down, vaguely forwards. Keep moving. Follow the line.

24

We don't get lost enough. Not because we have GPS systems and maps, not because we're surrounded by information telling us exactly where to go and precisely how to get there, but because we're scared of chaos and disorder. Scared of a world turned upside down, a world without those ever-present signs and directions telling us what to do next; the multiple-choice tick-the-box formality that is modern life. Isn't there a branch of self-help that encourages us to find ourselves by getting out there and looking? Looking in the places we haven't looked a thousand times before? 'Follow the line!'

When I was fifteen, between my loss of faith in the Mormon doctrines I'd been brought up with and the belligerent punk spirit I was about to stumble into, I discovered The Beatles. The front room of our family house in Burnley, a two-bedroom semi-detached somehow divided up to fit our family of six, boasted a colour television (still only three channels) and a fake teak stereogram. Up until then the TV had held sway; suddenly, for me, the record player, with its wobbly dials and centre spindle, took over. Over the next couple of years I began to spend my after-school hours down at the Record Exchange on Standish Street, where the reek of dust and mould, flimsy cardboard sleeves and thick plastic 'sleeve protectors' became the most intoxicating smell on earth. The sound of the shop's doorbell ringing as I entered practically had me salivating – I was naïve and untutored, but began to acquire a knowledge of modern music from record sleeves alone. Bob Dylan's sleeve notes. Frank Zappa's gatefolds. The illicit record covers that I'd read about in *Melody Maker*, all priced down and graded: *Blind Faith*, *Led Zeppelin IV*, *Hapshash & The Coloured Coat* (the first ever picture disc), Jimi Hendrix (the thrill of *Electric Ladyland*'s opened sleeve!), a dizzying rush of culture and nonsense, freaks and giants, magicians and clowns.

I started to collect The Beatles albums and singles, second-hand and marked down, opening up a world I didn't quite understand. Drugs, sex and pentatonic scales. And right in there, mixed up with all that fabulous Lennon wordplay and McCartney melody, was George's 'The Inner Light'. Bloody hell, it was weird. I was young, I loved football and clothes and I don't think I was ready for Eastern philosophy.

Set to the hum of harmonium, drone and tabla, Harrison sung words that he'd used almost verbatim from the *Tao Te Ching*:

Without going out of your door
You can know the whole world
Without looking out of the window
You can see the ways of heaven
For the farther one travels
The less one knows.
(Lao-tzu)

Quick, lift the needle. Skip it. Let's get back to that John Lennon one about warm guns and Mother Superior.

Here in America, in the cold snap of December, I'm watching my son Johnny, five months old, stretching and trying to sit, to stand, to move. Learning to drag himself along, and eventually, any day now, to crawl. Joseph J. Campos writes in his essay 'Travel Broadens The Mind':

'When infants begin to locomote voluntarily, they undergo an extraordinary psychological reorganization. The onset of prone progression, especially hands-and-knees crawling, is followed by a staggering array of changes in perception, spatial cognition, and social and emotional development.'

Move, discover, explore. It's an instinct, a part of our make-up. If we must run – as many of us must – then let's run to places where we'll make discoveries, where we'll learn. I don't think it's an exaggeration to say that every wild run is an education, a learning.

My rite of passage as a teenager was to dress differently, read poetry, hitch-hike to concerts in Manchester, anything to experience that unknown 'other'. Neither George Harrison, in his search for a release from the madness of fame, nor Lao-tzu, in his personal quest for spiritual enlightenment, could convince me as a Lancashire school-boy that I ought to sit on a big cushion, stay put and meditate. *For the farther one travels, the less one knows.* At that point in my life, along with every other curious 16-year-old pop fan I had, believe me, every intention of travelling the world and, indeed, going out of my door.

In 1976 Britain played host to a sharp rise in popularity of the neo-Nazi National Front party. At the same time as I was pondering George's call to passivity, a drunk Eric

Clapton was was witnessed by several thousand people onstage in Birmingham, urging his audience to vote for the ultra-right wing politician Enoch Powell and declaring that 'This is England, this is a white country!' His tirade – a lexicon of racial slurs (whatever he may have intended) caused a furore that led directly to the founding of a group called Rock Against Racism, and indirectly to my first involvement in politics. I went to an RAR benefit concert, bought a badge and wore it proudly on my school uniform. Racism – the very fact of it – just hadn't occurred to me before then. One of my best friends, Nadeem, was Pakistani; I'd stuck up for him when kids had hurled insults at him because he was my mate, not because I really understood what those insults meant.

The National Front began gathering, demonstrating and marching in Britain's city centres, and Rock Against Racism responded by holding concerts and rallies, provoking people like me into discovering the big, messy, contradictory world of politics. This was no time for meditating, obviously. In hindsight, Clapton's act of small-mindedness made me who I am, because it made me question my own small-town prejudices. As well as discovering a world of fields and hills outside Burnley, I felt pushed to discover a world of ideas, too. Wild running isn't just an escape *from* somewhere, it's also a route *into* somewhere. Somewhere much bigger, a place where John Muir and me can meet on uneasy ground, high up a mountain, and get a better view of the earth. It's a big place, frankly, and it's a better view from up here than from a stage in Birmingham.

While our cities get ever more populated, I can still head off and spend entire days running over this big revolving muddy ball and meet only animals and birds. The countryside is vast. Out there, I don't worry myself over finding pens that work, or replying to emails, or recording a TV programme. Our world is there to be found, to be explored, to be enjoyed. Beyond the streets and the houses, the offices, schools and bars that we know so well, are places we've never been to, out on the edges of our towns and cities. Wide-open spaces and tiny bolt-holes, landscapes as alien as planets, dark, tangled hiding places and horizons as broad as we'll ever see. And in those spaces – the places outside the confines of what we're told to do, and what we're shown as normal, and what to look at and what to eat and how to dress and where to run – are *'a staggering array of changes in perception, spatial cognition, and social and emotional development'*. Look through your window, go out of your door – heck, tie on some studded shoes and find yourself somewhere different to run – there's a lifetime's worth of exploration out there.

25

Joseph Priestley was born in 1733 in Fairhill, a small village eight miles south of my present home in Leeds, Yorkshire. A religious dissenter, he practised as a non-denominational minister in a chapel in the centre of Leeds while learning a trade as a chemist. This dual life, balanced precariously between ethics and science, between morality and truth, belief and knowledge, infused Priestley with an open and inclusive idea of the world; a great debater, he revelled in the world's contradictions and possibilities, and somewhere in that gap between his role as chemist and as preacher emerged a philosopher. As a chemist he discovered oxygen and nitrous oxide; he also invented both the pencil eraser and soda water. As a minister of the Unitarian Church he stirred up the conformist bigots and brutes with his dismissal of basic Christian tenets (he refused to believe in either the Trinity or the Devil), and as a philosopher he loudly supported social and political reform, praising the French and American revolutions.

In 1791, having moved to Birmingham with his wife and family, Joseph arranged a dinner to celebrate the anniversary of the storming of the Bastille in Paris. A mob, whipped up by government fear of the spread of revolutionary ideas to Britain, gathered to oppose the dinner, attacking those who attended and eventually forcing the Priestley family to flee their home, which the royalist crowd promptly burnt to the ground before going on a three-day rampage, torching religious dissenters' homes and chapels. All Priestley's laboratory work was destroyed, and when King George III was eventually forced to send troops to the area, he said dismissively: 'I cannot but feel better pleased that Priestley is the sufferer for the doctrines he and his party have instilled, and that the people see them in their true light.'

Under threat of arrest for 'seditious libel', Joseph Priestley and his family were forced to flee the country. They settled in America, in a small village overlooking Pennsylvania's Susquehanna River, and from there Priestley was able to live out his life corresponding with much-missed colleagues in England. He was often unhappy in exile; but as a radical and dissenting voice who had created a new life, free from the unenlightened prejudice he had suffered at home, he became an example to a small group of English poets and philosophers who heard of his situation. These poets and thinkers called themselves Pantisocrats (meaning 'government by all') and in 1794 they gathered to create a utopian scheme whereby twelve men and twelve women would emigrate to America and set up an egalitarian community on the Susquehanna, near to Priestley's home in Northumberland, Pennsylvania. The principle minds behind the whole scheme were Robert Southey and Samuel Taylor Coleridge, in the days before both would join Wordsworth on his mountainous treks in the Lake District. It was Coleridge who, in the main, saw both mountain walking and poetry as great adventures; who viewed life as a world of possibilities.

The Susquehanna River winds its way through Pennsylvania not in an indolent, quiet way but as a spectacular rush of plunging valleys, forested islands and cragged, bouldered hillsides. It drags with it the drama of natural chaos, settling occasionally at forks and widened expanses before resuming its headlong rush eastwards towards the Chesapeake Bay and the Atlantic. It's little wonder that the Pantisocrats viewed this area as a haven from the city-bound intolerance and jaundice of their literary circles – their scheme, which never came to fruition, involved them living completely independently, without personal property or government, with all possessions and labour given towards the common good.

Historically, philosophers, thinkers and idealists who are ridiculed and derided by the bigotry of conservatism and fear are labelled 'outcasts' – literally cast out, often (as in Joseph Priestley's case) physically, and frequently out of the cities and into the countryside. And the countryside, the world outside the hemmed-in ideologues of the city, welcomes them.

For a while, in the heart of the Yorkshire Dales, living in a rented house in a tiny village on a road that eventually petered out into the limestone hills, I clung to the idea that country people, like the countryside itself, would be welcoming and open. For the most part they weren't. They were suspicious and closed off, wary of the townies who presumably wouldn't be allowed to join the club because we'd no idea how to shear a sheep or birth a calf. It probably wasn't always like this; feasibly, decades of incomers buying second homes and pushing up property prices, misusing the land, polluting the rivers, quarrying the hillsides and laying waste to the forests have built up enough suspicion to make that legendary 'country haven' a thing of the past. And, yes, I've been shouted at by farmers while out running; farmers who in turn have added their own forms of misuse of the fields, woods and rivers to the litany of our gradual destruction of the world around us. The environmental group American Rivers named the Susquehanna 'America's Most Endangered River for 2005' as a result of the excessive pollution it receives. Most of the pollution in the river is due to excess animal manure from farming, agricultural runoff, urban and suburban storm-water runoff and raw or inadequately treated sewage.

In 1802, a while after his utopian scheme had fallen through, Coleridge went for 'a wander' in the Lake District that took in an ascent of Scafell Pike, the highest mountain in England. He was the first recorded person to climb to its peak; he did so not in an effort to stick a flag at its apex or assume for himself a place in mountain-climbing history but because he was following his nose up there, discovering, exploring, sensing the landscape – in the words of his biographer Richard Holmes, 'Coleridge was in effect inventing a new kind of Romantic tourism, abandoning the coach and the high-road for the hill, the flask and the knapsack'.

Coleridge's 'tourism' bore no relation to modern-day tourism of course – he was his own travel guide, using ill-drawn maps (actually, substitute 'ill-drawn' for just plain 'wrong') and heading up and down, over and across places simply to experience sensation; to find the unexpected and to be a part of it. His account of the descent from

Scafell Pike is a beautifully narrated description of a bloke suddenly finding himself up the creek without a paddle. In his account, he drops, ledge by ledge, from the summit towards Mickledore, a rocky corridor at the foot of the Pike's huge crag. Finding himself on what we now know as Broad Stand, he realizes that he has dropped too far from the ledge above to climb back up; and the next drop plunges down the valley to certain death. This 'step' in the crag face is part of the route of the twenty-four-hour Bob Graham Round, and is infamous among walkers and runners alike. Having read Coleridge's account of being stuck there, I felt in good company. Let me compare our notes. Here's Coleridge:

The stretching of the muscles of my hands and arms, and the jolt of the Fall on my Feet, put my whole Limbs in a Tremble, and I paused, and looking down, saw that I had little else to encounter but a succession of these little Precipices . . . I began to suspect that I ought not to go on, but then unfortunately tho' I could with ease drop down a smooth Rock seven feet high, I could not climb it, so go on I must and on I went . . . the next three drops were not half a Foot, but every Drop increased the Palsy of my Limbs – I shook all over . . . and now I had only two more to drop down, to return was impossible – but of these two the first was tremendous, it was twice my own height, and the Ledge at the bottom was so exceedingly narrow, that if I dropt down upon it I must of necessity have fallen backwards and of course killed myself. My Limbs were all in a tremble – I lay upon my Back to rest myself, and was beginning according to my Custom to laugh at myself for a Madman, when the

sight of the Crags above me on each side, and the impetuous
Clouds just over them . . . overawed me. I lay in a state of
almost prophetic Trance and Delight – and blessed God
aloud, for the powers of Reason and the Will, which remain-
ing no Danger can overpower us!

I arose, and looking down saw at the bottom a heap of
Stones . . . As I was looking at these I glanced my eye to the
left, and observed that the Rock was rent from top to bottom
– I measured the breadth of the rent, and found that there
was no danger of my being wedged in, so I put my Knapsack
round to my side, and slipped down as between two walls,
without any danger or difficulty . . . (Coleridge, letter to
Sara Hutchinson, August 1802)

And here are my own notes:

And then it was Broad Stand. Oh how we laughed. Picture
a freshly netted fish, slipped and slapped onto the bottom of
a boat, gasping for air and manically twitching. Despite
support from Rupert and Alan on the ledge above shouting
instructions and giggling uncontrollably while feeding a
bizarrely knotted rope down a big slab of rock, I quite
plainly 'Did the Flounder'. Geoff and Fred watched from
below as my body inched fitfully over the small rock wall.
Rupert laughed: 'Reel him in, quick!'

Recalling Coleridge, I announced that my fish-flapping
and general scaredy cat approach to Broad Stand were in a
fine tradition of Romantic Tourism. Alan thought I was
hallucinating and pulled harder on the rope, and eventually
I scrambled to safety, breathing heavily and clinging onto
the horizontal land as if it were an original Coleridge

manuscript. All I needed now, I thought to myself, blinking
upwards toward the crest of Scafell Pike, was some opium.
(Bob Graham Round report, 2005)

The northern banks of the Susquehanna set the scene for the previously mentioned Conestoga Trail Race, billed as 'the toughest 10-mile race on the East Coast'. Starting from the Pequea Creek campground, the race route climbs nearly 3,000 feet through heavy forest, taking in the Wind Caves (one of the largest tectonic caves in the eastern US) as well as some spectacular pinnacles overlooking the river. The entry form for the race includes the paragraph:

WARNING: This is NOT your standard 10-mile race. The footing is uneven at best, and can be dangerous. A fall is probable. An injury is possible. Insect bites, sprained ankles, lacerations, and broken bones are some of the possible hazards. There will not be medical teams immediately on hand and our insurance will not cover your medical bills. You are responsible for your own self. Do not enter unless you are willing to risk and assume responsibility for any injuries that you may incur.

Now, that's a race I have to do. In the event, despite the severity of its warning, the race is a joy. On the tough climb up through the scrambled rock track to the race finish I suddenly have an image of those twenty-four men and women, the Pantisocrats, those intellectual outsiders who were going to escape to this area and make it their home. Clearing trees, building houses, sharing work and possessions. 'Government by all.' And shortly after, having finished the race, I sit on a bench and chat to another runner who asks what I think of the area. It's beautiful, I tell him. Incredible. And fantastic for running. He tells me he spent some time in England – three years – but that all his running there was on the road. 'You've nothing like this over there though, I bet,' he adds. 'There aren't any mountains in England, are there?' And I think of my homeland's beautiful peaks and of Coleridge with his knapsack and finally, full circle, of Joseph Priestley, exiled here on the Susquehanna for speaking his mind.

26

Soaking our senses in the storms and sunbursts of the outside world is something we now have to learn. It comes naturally to kids, of course – when we convince a grumbling Maisy, my 8-year-old daughter, to 'go for a walk' with us, she quickly forgets to drag her feet when confronted by the supersized natural playground that is the local woods. She'll play, invent, create and lose both herself and her sense of 'cool' when she has a good whipping stick in her hand and a tree swing overhead. Watch this! Watch this! This place is stuffed with ideas, with possibilities. The world we leave at home, its comforts and entertainments, vanishes with the stomped puddle water.

Three people last year bought me Haruki Murakami's book *What I Talk About When I Talk About Running*. It's a running book that's decidedly not about training programmes and stories of demon-beating or race-winning, and presumably it looks like a book I'd like as a present. But, despite the thoughtful narrative, I struggled to get past the first couple of chapters. Just a few pages into the book, Murakami writes: 'I run every single day. Today I ran for an hour and ten minutes, listening on my Walkman to two albums by The Lovin' Spoonful.'

Then by page fourteen he's telling me that in July he ran

186 miles. All of them on the road, wearing his Walkman. It disheartens me so much that by page forty-eight, just as he's preparing for the New York City Marathon, I decide to drop out and let him run the rest of the book alone. I'll eventually finish the book and I'll be glad of its company. But I won't engage with it as much as I'd like to – how can I? The author is wearing headphones!

I've never understood the desire to listen to music while running. In cars, vans and tour buses, stop-starting along millions of miles of tours with Chumbawamba, I can sit back with my headphones and listen to various corners of my record collection, its hums, plucks, snarls and harmonies, all the while looking out of the window at countryside I wish I was running through. At times the soundtrack is perfectly matched to the surroundings; Philip Glass's *Koyaanisqatsi* in centre-city Tokyo, Irma Thomas's 'It's Raining' during a German Black Forest thunderstorm.

The Lovin' Spoonful – Murakami's soundtrack – had one notable hit, 'Summer in the City', a strange choice with its hot 'n' bothered put-down of the boiling city sidewalk, fiery as a mach head, the vocalist tense and irritated. I understand this need for musical accompaniment, of course, among the city streets' barrage of unwanted noise. There's an intellegant and irregular mess of sound that The Lovin' Spoonful can filter out – the thrum of cars, sirens, horns, whistles, the dislocated snatches of music at every storefront, the drunken yell, the ignored alarm, the squeal of brakes as a car throws you over its bonnet and onto the pavement.

Away from the madding crowd, out in the wild, there's a different kind of cacophony, but it's one worth switching

145

off your music and listening to. It ebbs and flows, comes and goes, rises and falls, and it's always the appropriate soundtrack. The long deep shhhhhhh of rain, the shpakkk of puddles, the zzzzzz of insects, the natural ah-oooooo-ing reverb of a cow calling its calf. The birds are always there, everywhere, inescapable, snatching at the silence. Rivers can hum, tinkle, swoosh or boom. And every sound fits so perfectly with the tap, splat, pad of feet running through it. Sometimes the distant city sounds are inescapable, and the long, filmic hoot of a train or deep bass rumble of a truck reminds us of the incessant, non-stop, can't stop, won't stop of our other lives. Lives away from these grounded, earth-bound sounds.

Finding the wild places isn't as easy as it used to be. The city spreads, if not physically then with sound and light (ever lay awake listening to the distant orchestra of motors and alarms? Ever try to see the stars in a city ablaze with electric streetlamps?). And because these ribbons of asphalt that we run on are so inhospitable, so unwelcoming, we put our fingers in our ears like children and shout 'NOT LISTENING NOT LISTENING NOT LISTENING!' And the cars and the trucks and the coaches, those too-busy adults, they just ignore us, go right by us, voom voom voom voom voom . . .

There's a motorway stretched like elastic across the northern Pennines, between east and west, long outstretched arms from the country's central nervous system. This motorway, the M62, connects Liverpool and Hull, seaports once linked by water, a vital trade route. For many years this river–canal link between the cities served as a passage for goods from Europe on their way to

America. One of the historical destinations in the United States was Philadelphia via the Delaware River, less than a marathon run from where I write this in Arden.

At the very top of the M62 – right at the highest section of motorway in the United Kingdom – is a communications mast, a rundown cafeteria caravan and a single-track bridge across the six-lane road. This place is called Windy Hill (brrr. Pull on an extra top and zip those leggings up before you set off). When in the UK I meet my friend Geoff here for a run every month or so, it being both equidistant to both of us and perversely inappropriate. We usually have to lean into gales while trying to pull on cagoules, surrounded by the thunder of articulated lorries and the Doppler whine of speeding cars. From this point on the motorway, all vehicles head downwards, left or right, east or west, this way or that – and every uphill throaty cough of the engine can now be unwound in a frenzied descent to somewhere or other. One rainy, blustery day in early summer we met here and set off on a three-hour run which took us immediately away from the road and over a cresting moorland rise. Within ten minutes, the booming, whirring noise of traffic had vanished. This bizarre phenomenon is always surprising; whenever we've run around here we've always been shocked by how quickly the thrum of 'the infernal internal combustion engine' can be smothered by a natural soil 'n' grass barrier.

This rainy midweek morning we headed off along tracks and across unpathed hillsides, around blustery reservoirs and up peat-bog hills. After a while we cut back and headed towards the M62's unnatural valley again, several miles downstream (vehicles like fish, quick and clustered) from Windy Hill. There's a farm there – Stott Hall Farm – situated between the east- and west-bound carriageways, the road splitting around it. A whitewashed, cow-muck-splattered island, with tunnels beneath each half of the motorway so the cattle can access the fields on either side. Urban myth (as opposed to rural myth, of course) has it that the owner of Stott Hall Farm refused to allow the road builders to cross his land, forcing them to circumnavigate his property. This is, sadly, untrue. Geological fault lines meant that the road had to split, allowing (or forcing) the farm to become islanded, stranded.

We crossed through the farm's umbilical tunnels to the other side of the roaring road, sweated up the hill at the other side, and again quickly became lost to the sound of the juggernauts, commuters and boy racers. The hillsides banked against the motorway and blanked out its sound – *muffled it!* – easily and effortlessly. We ran on an ancient trans-Pennine path, faintly marked with inscribed standing stones. This was the original M62, four feet wide and rich in a history of coffin-bearers, tinkers, hawkers and messengers – those original fell runners, carrying news and being tipped for getting there faster than others.

Almost at the end of our run, rain falling now as we crested a long grey-green bank to a whitewashed stone Ordnance Survey trig point, we passed three women carrying bottles of wine and wearing summer dresses and light jackets. They stopped us, happy and carefree and stomping along in the same direction we were headed.

'Now, can we trouble you [giggle] – I'm sure you two fit

148

young men will know. We're on our way to Marsden. Is this the way to Marsden?'

The woman talking was redheaded and smiling and wearing heeled shoes. Geoff and me looked at each other.

'Marsden?'

'Marsden. We've got the day off, see. We're nurses, and we're on strike. Union called us out. So we've come for a walk.'

One of the other women chipped in. She was younger, less confident.

'We got t'bus to Denshaw. We're from Oldham, see. Look, we're having a drink to celebrate the day off. Only we're a bit lost.'

The thing is, they weren't just a bit lost, they were utterly lost. Actually, they were heading the wrong way, in the rain, on Pennine moorland. We were a stone's throw from the wild landscape made notorious as the burial ground used by the Moors murderers, Ian Brady and Myra Hindley, between 1963 and 1965. Geoff and me, we laughed, and they laughed, and we were all laughing together. Yes, you're lost, we told them. And look, see, on this map, this is where we are – and this is where you want to be. It's too far to walk, in the rain, in heels. Drunk. Chances are you won't get there.

We took them, reorientated, along the path to where we were parked and Geoff drove them all to Marsden, a long way away, but at least they were warm and dry. And later, we tried to be high and mighty about their lack of preparation, the danger they exposed themselves to. We tried, but we couldn't – it was just funny in the end. They wanted to celebrate a day off, they got off a bus in the countryside, and they started walking, with a couple of bottles of wine, no map and no raincoats. It's stupid, and silly, but in my book (in this book) isn't this underplanned wanderlust, this headstrong and foolish adventuring somehow more noble, more laudable than listening to The Lovin' Spoonful in the confined channel of a city street, somewhere, anywhere?

Nineteen seventy-nine, Lake Pontchartrain Bridge, New Orleans. It was the venue for the Mardi Gras Marathon: the course was a last-minute replacement for the traditional course, necessitated by a sudden strike by the city's police force. The new course wouldn't need traffic control, as it was to be run almost entirely on the Lake Pontchartrain Bridge. The bridge is over twenty miles long, and straight as an arrow. Participants would set off a few miles shy of one end of the bridge and finish pretty much at the other end. One road, no bends, nothing to look at but the end, somewhere in the distance. On a clear day, the horizon (for someone around six feet tall) is around three to four miles distant. Imagine that, watching the road bridge in front of you rolling out, step by step, for two, three, four, five hours. If you thought Manhattan's First Avenue was bad, try this. That was 1979, the year the Sony Walkman went on sale in the US.

27

So much of the language of the marathon is about pain. The race is almost completely internalized, to the point where a description of a runner's marathon can take you through every step of the twenty-six miles without incorporating any of the detail of the surroundings, the streets, the buildings. You'll be lucky if you get a weather report tossed in. Marathon narratives are all about fatigued legs, nausea, exhaustion, aches, cramps and strains. And the wall! Always the wall. The marathon is an ordeal, rarely a joy. Oprah Winfrey famously decided to run a marathon, asserting throughout her training that willpower and a positive spirit would ensure she completed the race. Her words on finishing? 'I'm never going to run another marathon.' The race is a challenge, nothing more. A trial, a test of will.

Marathon running is a terrible experience. Monotonous, heavy and exhausting.' (Veikko Karvonen)

There's something to be said for testing your limits, pushing yourself so hard it hurts. Getting out of the comfort of the everyday, reaching for experiences that aren't just easy, or handy, or effortless. As a kid I read about Captain Webb, smeared head to toe in porpoise oil and braving jellyfish stings and heavy currents to swim the English Channel (his zigzag route was over thirty-nine miles long). They say he was fortified during the swim by occasional glugs of brandy. As we approach middle age (whatever age that might be nowadays – years, like minutes and hours, speed up and slow down) we remember these heroic daredevils in their flimsy costumes, flexing their muscles in our childhood daydreams, and we think: I can do something, too. I can. I'll show the world what I can do. We look around at the options, and, unwilling to smear ourselves in fish oil, we opt for the most conspicuous and straightforward challenge available to us. The city marathon.

Of course we won't enjoy it. It will be agony. And it will probably be boring, indescribably so (which is possibly why so few marathon runners describe the world around the race, focusing instead on their personal, painful battle to cross the finishing line without chucking up). But it's there, and all it takes is a bagful of fancy running gear from the sports shop at the mall, plenty of willpower and one of those books explaining exactly what you have to do to complete a marathon (there are lots to choose from).

Thus the intention, the training and the race itself are all internalized. There's little thought about the actual context of the marathon (other than an obsession with ultra-flat courses and plenty of drinks stations), only on the self. This is not a race against other people, it's a race against me. I will hate it. But I will do it, so that I can say, 'I ran a marathon'. The pain is part of the package, obviously – hence the long-standing runners' slogan, 'No Pain, No Gain', an idiom I have always hated. What, you can't get better at something if it isn't painful? That's not only gruesomely discouraging, it's also not true. If you enjoy something, you tend to do it more. And you get better at it. When I first raced downhill as an adult, from the top of Burnsall Fell in my very first hill race, I was scared stiff. The summit was surrounded by broken shale, loose rock, peat bogs and tufts of heather, a complication of hazards and trip-ups. But as I launched myself tentatively into the descent, I discovered something: I loved it. I was captivated in that instant. Others came flying past me, hurdling the rough ground and bounding down the hillside while I jogged gingerly towards the safety of the open fields. But I knew there and then that this was something I wanted to do, again and again.

The more I ran on rough ground, the better I became, especially at downhill racing. Scree-running, sliding down muddy banks and sodden grass, hopping through crags and loose earth. I loved it all, found it exhilarating. Sheer joy. 'No Pain, No Gain' only works because it rhymes and it's short. So we can all understand it. Douglas Barry, formerly head of the Irish Mountain Racing Association, describes how 'running up and down a mountain isn't just any old 10K road race. It's an adventure, a taste of excitement. A defying of gravity!' As a slogan, that statement doesn't work. How do you fit that onto a T-shirt? But it beats 'No Pain, No Gain' for me every time.

Wild running can be hard, painful, grin-and-bear-it tough. But by its nature – and by its very placing *in* nature – it can never be solely about pain and discomfort. It also has to be about the world around us as well as the world inside our heads. It externalizes running. Places it outside the mental battle going on in your skull, outside the me-me-me. A city marathon can hardly help but internalize, since the external is so oppressive; hemmed in by tall buildings, cordoned off and guided, with volunteers handing you drinks and sponges, hundreds of other feet to follow (as well as that line down the middle of the road) – where else is there for your thoughts to go but inwards? Which might go some way to explaining the self-helpish tone of so many of the books on marathon running.

28

I first started to play music around the age of sixteen, on a cheap Spanish guitar with nylon strings. It was my mum's, and she'd bought it to take guitar lessons – I think she lasted two months – at which point the guitar just stood there, leaning against the living-room wall, looking at me with its sad untuned strings until I picked it up. I'd bought a record by so-called 'punk poet' Patrik Fitzgerald called 'Safety-Pin Stuck in my Heart': three chords and an acoustic guitar. And this was punk, so of course I thought, 'I could do that'. And this was punk, so I had friends who couldn't play either, but who also thought, 'I could do that'. And this was punk, so we formed a band and called ourselves Chimp Eats Banana (after some graffiti sprayed on a bus shelter in Burnley. Isn't that how all bands get their names?). The first thing we did wasn't to desperately learn 'Freebird' or 'Smoke on the Water', or even 'Anarchy in the UK'. The first thing we did was sit round working out how we could be different from everyone else. What we could sing about that nobody else was singing about. We'll use theatre! We'll dress up! We'll play songs with weird time signatures that we weren't good enough to play!

From the start it was an adventure. That's probably an overused word in this book, but it's the word that nag nag nags away at my life, from music to running. In Chimp Eats Banana we set out to do something different, refused to follow the set pattern, took what was expected and messed it up, bent it, played with it. It's only while writing this book that I've come to see my running – wild running – as an expression of that wilful desire to play. Chimp Eats Banana were awful, but entertainingly so. Of course we couldn't play well enough to articulate our ideas, and it took me a year to master those three Patrik Fitzgerald chords. At our first live concert, someone handed me an electric wire attached to my guitar and told me to 'plug into the amp'; I stood there on stage, in front of 100 people in the upstairs room of a working-men's club, holding the end of that wire for dear life and not having a clue where to put it. It didn't matter. We were a noisy, messy, funny thing and that's what we aimed for. We would never get a record deal or play on TV but we'd scramble our way through rehearsals and concerts trying to come up with something strange and original.

I never did learn to play 'Freebird', any more than I learnt to accept that running on pavements was the limit of my running horizons. When Chimp Eats Banana split up as its members went off to college or work, I began to practise playing guitar more seriously and learnt how to write and structure songs; discovered harmony singing, record production, all the nuts and bolts of being in a band. But the seed of playfulness had been sown, and by 1981 – the year we started Chumbawamba – any band I played in was never going to be just another rock 'n' roll band. That was the year I ran the marathon, and the year I dropped out of education for good.

156

By then, having dropped out of two college courses, twenty years old and able to pack my entire possessions into two rucksacks (one clothes and shoes, the other vinyl records), I found myself living in a barely habitable squat in Leeds and setting up a communal-living situation with six or seven other anarchists, artists and musicians. The house had been left empty and vandalized – anything of any value (doors, light fittings, locks, the stair banister) had been stolen before we moved in and the majority of us lived on unemployment benefit payments and part-time jobs. I was scruffy-looking (a legacy of recalcitrant northern English punk and its stubborn hatred of London style) and had stopped going to the barber's, taking scissors to my own hair. We shared a dog called Derek and several cats. Frankly, as far as anyone could see, I was a hippy. I'd dropped out.

I hated this. I hated the idea of 'dropping out' and I hated that people might see what I did as 'dropping out'. I'd tried studying graphic art (designing boxes of spaghetti and soap); I'd worked hard for a year at the university learning Chaucerian English (largely unfathomable, uninteresting and, worst of all, utterly useless); and my stint at the post office ended when I realized that the job my grandad had stuck at for almost his entire adult life was liable to clamp itself onto me and not let go, ever. I hadn't left these institutions out of failure or fear but out of boredom, out of an overwhelming sense of wanting to do something interesting with life. To grab it, direct it, make it mine – not submit to it. So here I was, determined and energized and (according to the locals in this run-down area of West Leeds called Armley) living at 'the big house with the hippies up the road'.

I didn't want to create alternatives, become separate. I didn't want to cut myself off. I wanted to shock, amuse and provoke, sure – wanted people to notice me, even if it was only to laugh – but I refused to see myself as apart from the world. Germaine Greer dismissed 'the dropout' as someone who 'pillages intricate and demanding civilizations for his own parodic lifestyle'. I took this to heart – I wanted to be in a band that worked hard and created things on its own terms. Not just for 'fun' (though it is fun) but because it could be the thing that put me in the world, that gave me a voice. I'd watched Leeds bands rehearse and I'd been shocked by the lackadaisical, half-arsed attitude to what I consider a privilege – to be able to make music with other people, to write songs, to play them for other people. I'd watched the spliffs being passed around and the rehearsals turn into jams. Long-winded, cyclical and dull as ditchwater, melodies and tunes and bits of lyrics coming and going before anyone had a chance to jump on them and capture them, write them down, remember them, work with them.

I was young and naïve, freshly discharged from the waste pipe of my education and eager as a puppy to play – what I'd learnt from punk was a belligerent self-belief, a tearing up of the past, and a fundamental creed of social responsibility. That meant sticking with the world and being part of it, not disappearing into a subculture of escapism; it also meant no jamming. When Chumbawamba began to take shape, our rehearsals were disciplined as well as enjoyable and creative; they were inclusive and didn't exist without a point (to write songs). We didn't spend our time doing LSD and magic mushrooms – we had songs to write. We stuck up enormous sheets of paper on the walls, filling them with song structures and chords. We discussed, laughed, made plans, and laughed some more. No one played the blues. No one played solos ('You know how much I hate solos!' said Ringo Starr).

Why all this talk of hippies and dropouts? Well, in that early 1980s squatted hiatus, when what became Chumbawamba first moved en masse into that big Victorian house, it felt like I'd just spent three years of my life shaking off the post-hippie hangover. My generation was raised on The Bee Gees and Genesis, so punk's joyful glee at rejecting the millionaire superstar death rattle wasn't something to feel complacent about. Because, given half a chance, they'd all hide their platform-soled silver boots and pretend they'd been cool all along... Meanwhile, in the larger world out there, Margaret Thatcher was setting up her stall as hellish sorceress of the free market (hero of the haves against the have-nots) and I was falling headlong into a decade of part-time jobs, self-made cassette tapes and printing-press pamphlets. It was a strange time, and a time for fighting the urge to disappear into one of those sub-cultural bolt-holes; a time not to run away but to stake a claim in the everyday.

The first London Marathon was held in 1981. It was in all the newspapers – former Olympian Chris Brasher, after a visit to the New York Marathon two years earlier, brought mass-participation road-running to Britain. Over 6,000 runners raced around London's streets in a rough approximation of what Brasher had described (talking of New York's race) as 'the greatest folk festival the world has seen'. That is, if you discounted New Orleans' Mardi Gras, Rio's

Carnival, and countless other well-known and hugely attended traditional festivals around the world. Brasher's gushing description of the New York City Marathon also included the report that 'last Sunday, 11,532 men and women from 40 countries in the world ... laughed, cheered and suffered'.

This suffering came not only to our capital city but to the north of England – just five months after this land-mark London race, Bolton, in Lancashire, hosted the larg-est European marathon ever run, with 8,000 runners. This is where we came in, with DJ Jimmy Savile and myself in Bolton joining those 8,000 laughing, cheering, suffering runners. I don't actually remember much suffering. Tiredness due to undertraining compounded by the unyielding roads and my crappy shoes, perhaps. No, this was an attempt to drop in, rather than out. Try something new, something big and exciting. It didn't turn out like that. Sadly, I had to chalk up running as something else I'd dropped out of, along with the Chaucerian English and art school spaghetti boxes. (I just didn't suffer enough.)

I'm still unclear, a quarter of a century after the event, why watching my first fell race, several years after that marathon, should have had such an impact, why it was so different. By that time, tumbling happily towards the end of the eighties with all its detestable me-me-me culture, I wasn't particularly looking for something to do. I was busy with at least three jobs as well as continuing to write, sing and tour with the band. I was in a relationship, didn't drink or take drugs, and didn't have an ounce of excess fat on me. I can think of only one reason why I may have fallen so hard for fell running – it looked like fun. The kind of surging, primal fun I didn't experience during that marathon in Bolton. Those fell runners, throwing themselves down hillsides – they looked like people at play. There may have been suffering, but it certainly wasn't in evidence; on the contrary, I saw no martyrdom and torment, only satisfaction, humour and genuine joy. Why I pinpoint this as a reason for my wholesale conversion to trail and hill running is that, quite simply, it still makes me feel like this; every day.

And the young man who was looking for a place in the world, the dropout with a fear of being seen as a dropout – he found a way to connect with the earth, with actuality, with the hard-nosed, absolutely dropped-in stuff that is now. Making that connection opened up a macrocosm of physical and metaphysical paths and trails, all leading outward to other people and other places. This earth that is being crippled and curdled by excess and war, that is being used up and spat upon by corporations and governments, this is not an abstract political earth, rotating as a graphic on news programmes and floating, helium-borne, over peace marches; this is the same earth that splashes and slips beneath my feet. That grabs me and pulls me down to its level, sometimes, laughing at my grazed hands on its paths and at my panting face in the wet grass, that opens up and declares its dusks and dawns, its tangles and its plains.

Coming off Blencathra during my 2005 Bob Graham Round, high above the twinkling 2 a.m. lights of Cumbria 3,000 feet below me, I could see to the east the faintest glow of the sunrise over the Pennine hills. As I clambered, skipping lightly down the easier sections while gripping

161

tightly at each rocky impasse, I watched the glow spreading outwards and upwards, flooding the dark meadows and darker-still river valleys with a red-turning-burnt orange, an orange-turning-deep yellow, a yellow with a heart of absolute white. The middle of this one night, twenty minutes of a picture show, a once-only performance; tomorrow would be different. This was the stuff that rooted me. There's no dropping out of this. Who could be up there, seeing what I was seeing, and not feel kinship with this big old ball of clay we take for granted?

29

I'm an anarchist. I mistrust authority; I believe that I can be responsible enough to act both without being told what to do and without telling other people what to do. Beyond this, definitions become tangled and open to change and challenge – anarchism doesn't have a defining position, nor do I want it to have. Just as the world changes, so must our ideas change to compensate and accommodate. I'm not fastened to the words of some long-dead political philosopher, just as I'm not determined to run along the same path every day. I run, and I may turn left, or right, or go straight ahead, and often I don't know until I get there. Often I don't know where a trail leads, only that it is up or down – so I choose, and then right around the next corner it goes somewhere else, somewhere unexpected.

Guy Debord, anarchist film-maker and writer, practised a roughly structured way of discovering the truth about a place through a concept named dérive, translating roughly as 'drift'. Originating with the French Letterists of the 1940s, it announced a new way of seeing the world, and boasted an academic name – *psychogeography*: exploring an environment by aimlessly strolling, drifting, without preconceptions, and understanding that world through a concoction of geography, senses and emotion. What's inside affecting what's outside, and vice versa. The French philosopher Merleau-Ponty, around the same time as the Letterists, was proposing that our bodies – through touch, taste, smell, etc. – were embedded in the world, not separate from it. That we are co-natural with the world. And hill walker Nan Shepherd, in her beautiful prose-hymn to the Scottish Cairngorms, *The Living Mountain*, writes that we are beginning to forget that physical, bodily experience of our world: '. . . its spaces, textures, sounds, smells and habits'.

In Debord's case this world was urban, his strolls being along city streets. By 'following one's nose', he and his fellow Situationists aimed to find a 'totality' of ideas about that city, wandering into and out of danger, being excited and bored, always coming across something new to confront and be confronted by. He'd be appalled at the city marathon, for sure, with its endless lines of traffic cones (those small plastic orange orderlies, pushing you back in when you want to get out) and its obvious similarity to herding sheep. Running a marathon not only disallows you from understanding where you are, it actively prevents it by creating an entirely new, wrapped and sealed environment. A city within a city. An extra set of barriers and walls within the already existing ones. I can think of little less conducive to the enjoyment of running than this. It is the anti-dérive, the mockery of any search for truth and ideas.

Hand in hand with my political philosophy of off-road running is its base nature, its absolute primitivism: the primal urge to run (as hunter-gatherers) and for that running to be outside, in the wild. I don't want the intervention of the state in my running; the less I have to deal with permits and traffic control the better. I want my runs to escape the tangle of commerce, law and permission, want to feel like I've jettisoned the weight of expectation and demand.

Not that running away from the city roads needs to dovetail into a runner's ideas on politics and culture – conversely, it can be a release from those ideas. A way of finding some sense of freedom from the narrowing confines of that everyday barrage of attitudes and theories. Or possibly offer just a space broad and high enough to think properly, to think without the weight of the urban/suburban straitjacket.

And then again (again), maybe running on the forest tracks and mountain paths is just plain, simple, natural fun.

'People must not do things for fun. We are not here for fun. There is no reference to fun in any act of Parliament.' (A. P. Herbert, British politician)

Thor Gotaas's book *Running: A Global History* is both a comprehensive and whistle-stop dash along the cultural and social timeline of running. Beginning with the South American Inca messengers of the 1500s, it clarifies the nature of cross-country running (sometimes literally across entire countries) as an important part of our social history. The Inca athletes would run distances of up to sixty miles, over mountain passes and along ill-developed roadways, carrying messages, gifts and news. They ran in relays and could cover almost 200 miles in twenty-four hours – significantly, much faster than the invading Spaniards' horse-mounted messengers.

Even earlier than this were the foot messengers of Central Europe, runners who could cover long distances on foot over rough terrain. In return they were paid good wages and excused military service; it was to be 200 years before the roads were good enough for horses to make faster progress than humans. During this time, the fat and lethargic landed gentry of Europe's aristocracy chose their favoured runners carefully, hastening their own early deaths while employing the fittest, healthiest young men as their 'running footmen'. These runners were kept in much the same way as a rich man then kept racehorses. Gotaas relates a story told by Montague Shearman in his book *Athletics and Football*:

> *On one particularly warm day the applicants* [for the job of running messenger to the Duke of Queensbury] *were running backwards and forwards in uniform for the duke while he was lying back indolently on the balcony. He liked one of the men in particular and, happy to see such a fine fellow, made him carry on for a long time. Finally the duke called: 'That's enough for me', at which the runner pointed at his smart, borrowed uniform and shouted back, 'This is enough for me', and ran away too fast for anyone to catch him.*

Being employed by the aristocracy to run errands was commonplace until well into the twentieth century, and trench runners – soldiers whose job it was to run between posts relaying messages – were essential during the First

World War. (The young Corporal Hitler was himself a dispatch runner.) In the years before the war, wealthy Europeans liked to holiday at French spa resorts, and the Pyrenean village of Vernet-les-Bains became a hotspot for aristocracy and royalty such as Queen Victoria herself. Because the spa lacked any refrigeration, local runners were employed during the summer months to run to the top of Le Canigou (over 2,000 metres in height), gather a sackful of ice at the summit, and run back down again, a round trip of around thirty kilometres. For, since Vernet boasted a thermal spa, drinks were expected to be chilled. Of course.

But what started out as the serious business of carrying news and messages over distance, from breathless Phidippides to the postboys of rural Europe, gradually became a pastime, a sport. Horses could eventually travel long distances much faster than man or woman if shod frequently, added to which, being reined and blinkered, they had little opportunity to stop under a handy canal bridge for a nap and a cigarette. Back before all of this, at the eleventh-century Scottish Braemar Gathering, lads were already challenging each other to race up and down the local mountain. The practice had become commonplace by the seventeenth and eighteenth centuries, and by the mid-1800s many local fairs and feast days around Britain included an organized race out to the nearest summit and back. The English Lake District's villages all pride themselves on their annual sports day, some stretching back over 200 years. The tiny village of Grasmere, picture-postcard friendly and nestled around the banks of Grasmere lake, is famous for two things: as the home of William Wordsworth and as the home of the Grasmere Guides Race, run since 1852.

Wordsworth lived in a small cottage with his wife Mary and sister Dorothy, entertaining, for lengthy periods, Samuel Taylor Coleridge and Thomas de Quincey, opium addicts both. I have an image of Wordsworth, addicted gallivant and rambler, urging his friends on, stride by stride, up the nearby Rydal and Fairfield peaks – and, in turn, imagine Coleridge's insistence on stuffing the contents of the cottage's medicine cabinet into his knapsack. I raise two 'Kubla Khan's for your 'I Wandered Lonely as a Cloud'. Coleridge, in fact, was a keen and expert walker himself – as I've already mentioned, he was notably the first person to reach the summit of England's highest mountain. And even before he moved to Grasmere, Wordsworth had become in thrall to John 'Walking' Stewart, a philosopher who, as his name suggests, spent his days walking and thinking. Stewart earned his reputation by coupling his ideas on nature with walks across Persia, Arabia and Africa before his perambulations to, through and around every European country (including Russia). Much of his travels, in the manner of Debord after him, were aimless. Not quite dérive, but certainly, fascinatingly, bonkers.

Wordsworth, fired by Stewart's writing and his own fervent support for the French Revolution, walked with passion and purpose – his wasn't the casual stroll of the clichéd delicate poet-child but the dedicated stride of the pioneer, blazing a trail across the landscape: he declared walking (in particular, hill walking) an essential tool of his work. As Rebecca Solnit points out in her glorious book *Wanderlust*, 'For Wordsworth walking was a mode not of travelling, but of being'. Solnit points to Wordsworth's aversion to 'the deformities of crowded life . . .' and his celebration of not just the hills and valleys but of walking as a radical political act, an identification with the earth and with the poor and a marked, physical and symbolic disdain for the city-bound grandeur of nobility with its genteel, showy promenading.

Trail running is anything but 'showy' – it willingly gives the stage to the surrounding hills and valleys and instead plays the part of awe-struck audience. Encore! For many, one of the undeniable appeals of the city marathon is its staged flamboyance. The marathon is a very public affair, and there's usually an audience of many thousands to witness the whole show from Vaseline-rubbing prologue to vomiting finale; and, for the audience, a free all-ages circus featuring grimacing, waving clowns (sometimes literally, along with panto-mime horses, all sorts of animals and the odd 130-lb antique diver's suit*).

The carnival used to be an essential part of our lives, a ritualized celebration to mark the season's changes. Bonfires were originally 'bone fires', literally the burning of animal bones at the end of summer to ward off – and warn of – the oncoming frost. Bone fires were celebra-tions, feasts, staking claim to our survival through another cycle and heralding our gathering together in

---

* Lloyd Scott completed the 2002 London Marathon clad in a deep-sea diving suit. He finished the course in a record slow time of 5 days, 8 hours, 29 minutes and 46 seconds, raising £100,000.

the face of colder weather. In this fire, people saw off summer and shook a fist at winter; set a big blaze to measure the distance between harvest's gathering and seed sowing. With the bone fire, people tried to make sense of a world without the regular, ever-present tick-tock of modern time; the carnivals were unruly and, over time (regulated state time) they were restricted, diminished and replaced by Christian festivals and council-run spectacles (look but don't touch). In my hometown of Leeds, 70,000 people drive out once a year to the sprawling landscaped Roundhay Park to watch fluorescent-jacketed fire safety officers guard a bonfire built by council workmen from untreated, approved salvage timber. The fire is sponsored by the UK's largest customer management outsourcing company (sic) and the local commercial radio oldies station. And the local fires, which for so long have been part of community life, are disappearing, year by year, the beautiful tumbledown hodgepodge replaced by safety tape and hard hats and sponsors' logos, planted every few metres around the perimeter fencing. I bet those fences would burn a treat.

Festival time was a time to forget the restricted, sponsored and manufactured fun and be part of something spontaneous, muddled and untidy. And we yearn for these festivals, we love mass celebration – we need it – but festivals have stopped belonging to us; now they are presented to us with a cost of admission, a leaflet explaining the rules and a row of fast-food stands. The marathon is a joyful coming together, a celebration, a triumph of community and kinship – but it's also moderated, overseen and supervised in a way that usurps that carnival spirit. A history of merry-making sold back to us, at a price. Entry fee for the 2010 New York City marathon? $185. Unless you're a non-US resident, in which case it rises to $265.

30

The Arden house I'm sitting in as I write this belongs to a couple who've long since packed their bags and moved to America's West Coast. Cue footage of covered wagons heading off across the Great Plains, coupled with US Department of Agriculture film of smiling, freckled kids chomping on freshly picked oranges. Today they drop by, and we pass half an hour in polite conversation – they explain that winter for them is now the hottest time of year, and that their lives are lived permanently in shorts and sandals. How wonderful it is, they say. I'm nonplussed – no, bewildered – wondering why people like to escape the changing seasons. Are they escaping change? I can't say, of course – I'm from northern England, where the weather suits my temperament down to the muddy ground, where to wake up not knowing what the weather will be like adds to and feeds into a changeable temperament; or so my inner weatherman tells me, pointy stick in hand. Different days require different skies, landscapes clothe and reclothe themselves according to the time of day, month and year. That northern English sensibility, with its stoic sense of grin and bear it, will go with whatever is chucked at it – it doesn't yearn for those all-year-round freshly picked oranges and neither will it begrudge the fact that it can't have them.

The weather, and the seasons here on America's mid-East Coast, change dramatically. The weather has its perpetual drama; its scenery, its costume and its lines change from act to act, so thoroughly that the last one is quickly forgotten. The river valley woods I ran through in mid-October, ankle-deep in a camouflage-carpet of leaf fall, appear again three months later as the winter's snow-fall melts and vanishes. Those winter storms! Sometimes, in those tempestuous January lashings, the wind practically shouted at me as I ran – don't you dare be down here too long, because, believe me, I'll blow you right out again! The mosquitos that hibernated (the females are the ones to stick it through the winter) are sloooowly waking up, the river's rocks are still too damp and mossy to run over, and, what with the greying skies an' all, if it wasn't for the occasional snake and that pair of retreating wild turkeys, this could almost be England. And as I write all this, it changes. It changes underfoot and in the air and at every path's bend.

Ironically, a visit 3,000 miles away to the American West Coast in January is accompanied by rain, wind and those same grey English skies. I bring the weather with me, of course, in my bumbag. While we're staying in Berkeley, California, there's a trail race in the Redwood Park, Oakland, 20K around the single-track ups and downs that twist themselves around the magnificent trees. I can't resist quoting Woody Guthrie:

This land is your land, this land is my land
From California to the New York Island.

173

Having raced the trails on Staten Island, New York, it seemed perfectly balanced to race at California's Redwood Park, to find a trail runner's disjointed way of spanning Pacific and Atlantic. The country's too big to run it all, from state to state (I tend to think that those who aim to run a city marathon in each of the fifty states are running their opportunities away, reducing their view of this huge continent to a single, endless tarmac strip), but I can't miss the chance to run along to Guthrie's lyrics.

My initial puzzlement at American school kids' enforced daily reciting of the Pledge of Allegiance was tempered by the very same school children learning Woody Guthrie's 'This Land Is Your Land'. Though I doubt many teachers choose to include the often omitted verse:

As I was walkin' I saw a sign there
And that sign said no trespassin'.
But on the other side it didn't say nothin'!,
Now that side was made for you and me!

Britain's Right to Roam Act of 2000 gave access to areas of heathland and downland that had previously been out of bounds, in many cases owned by rich gentry who kept such land for grouse shooting. It's long been accepted that, since the 1932 mass trespass, when a large number of Manchester ramblers chose to ignore the 'No Trespassing' signs and simply walked en masse over their favourite Peak District moorland, fell runners in Britain tend to run on all such open (unfarmed) land, regardless of whether or not they are trespassing. As Guthrie says, the sign can only be read from one side, and as long as runners act responsibly and in adherence to the safekeeping of the land and its inhabitants then there's little that any landowners can do to stop them.

The 1932 mass trespass on Kinder Scout sounded a warning shot on behalf of a population who'd been unceremoniously herded from the countryside and forcibly relocated by dint of economic hardship during the Industrial Revolution. An uprooted people, stuffed into back-to-back housing and thrown into the mills and factories. As the cities grew denser and darker, landowners extended their reach across the countryside, fencing off areas as big as counties and installing gamekeepers whose job it was to keep the land free of those troublesome ordinary folk who might spoil a good day's shooting by taking a stroll or a picnic on the duke's land.

Dave Nesbitt, one of the original Kinder Trespassers, said, 'The only chance that a young person had of getting away from mucky Manchester and Salford, full of slums and smoke and grime, was for about a shilling or one-and-six, to come out here in the fresh air – and there used to be a mass exodus on a Sunday morning.' After some young walkers were turned back one Sunday from one of the Peak District summits, and undeterred by warnings to be cautious from the official rambling associations, the Manchester Ramblers decided to take action. Up until then, most ramblers' experience of walking alone or in small groups and meeting gamekeepers had been a private amusement, but this time it was organized as an explicitly political action.

On the day of the trespass the mass of walkers were met by gamekeepers and Water Board employees (hired brutes armed with legal papers and weighty sticks) who tried to prevent their ascent to the summits; undeterred, the walkers brushed these thugs aside and the trespass continued. On their return, five of the ramblers were arrested, charged, and – shockingly – imprisoned. Running up the paths and trails surrounding Kinder Plateau it's impossible not to reflect on that day, when the designated straight line of history was abruptly interrupted and smudged by the peat-clagged walking boots of a few hundred people who dared to challenge the status quo. Public sympathy for the prisoners and increasing acts of trespass (several weeks after the Kinder Trespass, an access rally over private land near Castleton attracted 10,000 supporters) forced the issue, leading eventually to the creation of open National Parkland. Nevertheless, land access is a continuing issue for runners and walkers alike. *Country Life* magazine concluded in 2010 that more than a third of Britain's land is still in the hands of a tiny group of aristocrats. A band of just 36,000 wealthy individuals – less than 1 per cent of the population – owns 50 per cent of our rural land.

From my house in Armley, Leeds, I run through unkempt, unpaved ginnels (the northern word for hidden back alleys, underused pedestrian passageways avoiding the built-up straight-line roads) down to Gott's Park, named after its creator, Benjamin Gott. Gott was an obscenely wealthy industrialist who owned the Armley Mills, in 1805 the largest wool-manufacturing mill in the world. It solidly straddles the canal and river, still imposingly grand despite years of neglect and decay, a towering stone-built monument to the Industrial Revolution. Gott built himself a mansion on the furthest reaches of the park, high on a hill and overlooking the mill around one mile distant. From his vantage point in an upper room, the rosy-cheeked tycoon would watch his hundreds of workers make their way from the cramped housing of Armley down the grassy lane leading to the factory, carrying lanterns to see their way in the pre-dawn gloom. Late in the evening he would watch them make the return journey in the dark. The lane became known as Lantern Lane, today an overgrown and hemmed-in path that bisects what is now a municipal golf course on Benjamin Gott's former land.

Running this route on dark winter mornings is, like running the route taken by the Manchester Ramblers up on Kinder, to run with history sticking to the soles of your shoes. A reminder of how land is owned, managed and (sometimes) reclaimed. Lantern Lane bears the weight of a million footfalls, male and female, young and old. Children as young as seven worked long hours in the mill, and records show how some lost lives and limbs in the machinery there. Skipping lightly between the remaining dry-stone walls of the lane it's easy, despite the growth of the trees surrounding the old mansion, to see the windows from which Gott would survey his kingdom, this fire-lit procession of beaten-down souls with their pockets stuffed with bread. The dark and untidy hedgerow's insect buzz, the morning's awakening bird chatter, my feet tramp-tramp-tramping through the wet leaves, all of it struggling for volume under the weight of the past. I can't ignore it, this feeling of place and time that stretches backwards and refuses to let me forget the incredible hardships of ordinary people. Thugs with clubs to stop you climbing a hill, the mill-owner watching over this miserable human march. *This land is your land, this land is my land?* Not yet it isn't. But for all those who've tramped down this soil in centuries past, there's a hum and thrum of life that bursts from the earth and demands that these modern-day feet acknowledge the history of the land, and its people, that we run over.

> *Walking high upon the hills*
> *Rough-shod against well-heeled*
> *A butterfly breaks upon the wheel*
>
> *A compass and a cap*
> *A sing-song and a scrap*
> *A dotted line across the map*
>
> *All your week you were someone's slave*
> *Today you're a free man*
> *If they tell you, 'You can't' –*
> *Then you can.*
> (Chumbawamba, 'You Can')

31

Nineteen eighty-six. The biggest single of the year was Falco's 'Rock Me Amadeus', football's World Cup was being played in Mexico, and it was five years since DJ Jimmy Savile and myself had run the Bolton Marathon. In that five years, the flamboyantly tracksuited TV personality had run more than thirty marathons. I'd barely run a step. In the meantime, my dad – always a keen photographer – had taken up watching the traditional fell races around Lancashire, taking pictures of wiry blokes racing up and down the local hills at Hameldon, Thieveley and Pendle. He had a fair old collection of slides (remember them?) and one of those pointer torches. 'See that? That's a runner called Kenny Stuart. Best mountain runner in Britain. And look, on this one, see – that's him again, at Thieveley, racing a chap called Jon Wild. What a battle they had that day. Let me tell you all about it—'

In the interests of bolstering a fragile father–son relationship he convinced me to meet up with him in Skipton, an ancient Yorkshire town boasting a dilapidated castle and a canal full of hand-decorated barges, and drive out to watch an evening race in the northern Dales called the Simon's Seat Fell Race. When we got there it was raining, cold and muddy, but I was touched and amused by the utter lack of frills: the race registration was in a barn, and cows and horses made their displeasure felt at having their space taken over by scrawny, half-naked runners. At 7.30 the 200 or so bodies huddled together in the starting field a mile upstream from a twelfth-century Augustinian Abbey – men and women of all shapes and sizes, and notably, one of them sporting a pink Mohican haircut – before setting off at the sound of a blown whistle. Away they went, up into the smudged heavens, through the woods and out towards the top of the ridge. Mist, gloom and a twisting route up the hillside meant that the runners all but disappeared from view for around forty minutes, on up towards the looming, darkening slabs of Simon's Seat itself, a craggy summit that kept watch over the winding valleys below, looking for all the world as if it had tightened a thick grey raincoat around itself as the drizzle turned inevitably (this was Yorkshire, after all) into a downpour.

We waited. And waited. Until someone shouted, heralding a flurry of activity, claps and calls – and here were the runners now, hurtling down the finishing field, muddied to the eyeballs. And in the lead, bizarrely, was the lad with the pink Mohican haircut, a big grin on his face as he crossed the line, muddied and grubby but looking as if he'd barely broken sweat.

That was Gary Devine, who I got to know later as a local Leeds punk. He played bass guitar in a band, and wore his fingerless leather gloves even onstage. A few weeks later, at a concert up at Leeds University's Student Union building, I tentatively approached him and asked him about this fell running lark; he invited me to join him for a run one evening from his rented flat in Leeds' Hyde Park area. And it was in this meeting, this connection between punk and fell running – one culture I knew well and another I didn't – that I discovered a place where you could be athletic and fiercely competitive as well as maverick, funny, weird and individual. Where runners seemed to run right back to that place we try to label as 'childlike', a world of spattered mud and snot, hands-on-knees slopes, grabbing tree branches and sliding on your arse down rain-soaked grass. A place where a pink Mohican haircut can trump a standard short back and sides, where the kids who'd used school cross-country as an excuse to dawdle under a canal bridge smoking might find some of the joy and delight that institutionalized sport had left behind.

That first time, wearing football shorts and borrowed running shoes ('. . . to see if I like it. I'm not buying any until I know if I like it') I knocked on Gary's door and he appeared dressed in what struck me as a tight-fitting clown's outfit, all multicoloured and shiny. Welcome to the world of running gear, a land without shame. We headed off along Leeds' side streets and hidden ginnels and alleyways, coming out suddenly onto the edge of the heavily wooded side of Meanwood Valley. Paths crisscrossed up, down and along the ridge, and we headed off northwards to where the woods occasionally made way for roads and housing developments, a slaughterhouse, a cricket field. Eventually we were in open parkland, but instead of a steady jog across the lawned grass we were soon diving back into woods, further north, twenty minutes now and Gary realizing he was obviously going half as fast as he might normally be running without me in tow. All the while I was thinking, *'How come nobody told me about this?'* This upside-down, inside-out version of running where the streets and roads are just passing distractions in a search for those places where the running is dirty and uneven, where the world's natural disorder sparkles and rushes, bends and cracks. Running without blinkers on. We turned up into a brambled, wild place, trees and small rivers, disused buildings, climbs and descents. On and on and eventually back around, retracing our steps over bridges and down backstreets until we were at his front door, and while I gasped like some old Yorkshire coalminer he looked like he was yet to set off.

'Right, there's a race on Saturday if you're interested.'

'Erm [pant, pant] yeah, I'm interested. Where is it?'

'Burnsall, up in the Dales. It's only a mile and half long.'

A mile and a half. Should be easy.

'We'll pick you up at Eddie's Garage, on Kirkstall Road. You might need some different shoes.'

'Right.'

'See you then, then.'

I did the Burnsall race, finding out on arrival that the race climbs almost 1,000 feet to Burnsall Fell summit in its measly mile and a half, with the descent from the top being a sheer hurtle down scattered, strewn rock culminating in a five-foot dry-stone wall which has to be clambered up, grappled with and toppled over before a headlong rush through deep heather and steeply descending fields to the finish line. I was still wearing borrowed road-running shoes, which I discovered are next to useless on the slippery grass, sharp stone and uneven heather underfoot. The cushioning in road-running shoes – the wedge of rubber between the sole of your foot and the sole of your shoe – means you're not easily able to 'feel' what's under your foot. In off-road running, these shoes prompt you to rock around as if doing some particularly modern dance, unable to make a connection between your moving body and the changing earth beneath you. Add in the welter of padded support around the ankles of most road-running shoes and you have what appears to be a well-armoured defence against feeling anything at all, other than an inch or so of bright white, logo-emblazoned superiority over the humble green grass that you stand on. Or fall on, in my case, several times, both going up and coming down Burnsall Fell. Everyone around me in the race appeared to be wearing nothing but light slippers, to the underside of which were glued rubberized hedgehog skins. Very little in the way of ankle support, anti-pronating soles, heel counter-balances, comfort-padded ortho-tongues or very much of anything robust and supportive at all. Despite my complete exhaustion, I finished the race somewhere well down the field knowing I'd learnt more about the ground beneath my feet than about the lack of air in my lungs.

Feet have evolved to move over rough ground, sometimes shod but often bare. What feet clearly haven't evolved to do is suffer the repetitive impact of road running, and specifically to run over twenty-six miles on asphalt and concrete. Hence the glut of ways in which running-shoe manufacturers have sought to lessen the degenerative effect of those repeated heel strikes, that shuddering thump of a leg – all that delicate and fragile physiognomy – against a surface built to withstand twelve-wheel trucks carrying three-ton payloads.

The word pavement comes from the Latin '*pavimentum*', meaning trodden-down or beaten floor. But the pavement refuses to be trodden down; the pavement instead beats down the tread of our shoes. In a battle between foot and pavement, pavement wins. Trail runner Adam Chase says: 'The road to injury is paved', quietly echoing a global history of runners' shin, foot, knee, hip and back complaints.

In the year 1900 there were only ten miles of paved road in the United States. By 2005, the United States had the largest network of roadways of any country with 6,430,366 kilometres (3,995,644 miles) of the stuff. Early eighteenth-century builders and designers experimented with the use of layers of stone, earth and gravel as road-building materials but it wasn't until the innovative work of John McAdam in mixing stones with tar (creating tarmacadam) that truly modern road surfaces were created, if only (at that point) for the wheels of horse-drawn carriages. But still the road wasn't tough enough; in the 1870s, Belgian-born professor Edward de Smedt created the first 'maximum-density' asphalt, suitable for the battering it would receive from motor vehicles. The first use of this road asphalt was along Fifth Avenue in New York City; from 1976 onwards, the route of the New York marathon has incorporated almost three miles of Fifth Avenue.

The earth, in contrast to pavement and asphalt, has 'give'. It gives. It moves, it shifts, it bounces back. Like us, it evolves and reinvents itself daily according to circumstance – see how plants lie flat, spring to life, turn towards the sun, repair themselves. Resilient and strong, but, by design, changeable. The earth gets drenched, dries out, softens and hardens. And when I run across the hard, smooth surface of the rocks in the river, I'm aware that each one is at a different angle, each offering my feet a different platform. Tilting, falling, firm, wobbling, anything but repetition.

'Better die than live mechanically a life that is a repetition of repetitions.' (D. H. Lawrence)

32

At the risk of repeating myself, there's a great quote by record producer Nile Rodgers that Chumbawamba somehow didn't take to heart – 'Any real record person knows that the number one most powerful marketing tool when it comes to music is repetition.'

Chumbawamba followed what I can only describe as a wild trail of a career. Plenty of twists and turns, ups and downs, falls and scrapes – but definitely no repetition, much to the disappointment of our various record companies. Our one hit single ('I Fall During a Particularly Bad Descent, But I Get Up Again') took us several times around the world for a couple of years, a time when my running in particular suffered. Not that I'm complaining, you understand.

Nineteen ninety-eight, the band arrived in Miami, Florida, for a concert during Spring Break week and the temperature was soaring. We were booked into a hotel two or three blocks from the ocean, with two hours to seize before soundcheck. I changed into my running clothes, switched on the TV. The weather forecast told me it was over 100°F out there. Early afternoon and there was no breeze, very little shade and I was hatless. I couldn't do it. I'm a pasty-face, what the Scots once called a 'peely wally', fair-skinned, untanned and untannable. In that kind of heat I just burn. Sweat, burn and go red. But I needed to stretch, to run, and there was a hotel gym, and (as I'd done several times before) I gritted my teeth and decided that running on a treadmill would do me more good than spending the pre-soundcheck hours dozing off to MTV.

I went down to the gym and saw that Chumbawamba vocalist Dunstan was already there, sitting on a bike machine pedalling regularly and reading an international edition of the *Guardian*. Dunstan knew gyms. He even liked gyms. He could read the paper, watch the sports bulletins and do the crossword, all the while pedalling along on a bike that wasn't going anywhere. He was good at this; he had enough focus to make it a routine. Not me. I'm like a child, easily distracted and always wondering what's around the next corner. I found a running machine (even the words don't make any sense to me. Running and machine? One is natural, a journey, the other automated and fixed) and stepped on it. Dials, buttons, LED displays. I set it to *Hard*. Thirty minutes. There was a setting for 'hills'. Really. When set to 'hill', the treadmill beneath my feet began to rise, whirring and heaving until it reached a gently inclined gradient.

Hard. Thirty minutes. Come on, concentrate. I set off, settling into a pace and feeling inquisitively at the rubber treadmill under my feet, ridged and pliant. There were music videos on the TV up to my left and I determined not to watch them. Don't look at the dials, the LED, the television, the other people in the room. Concentrate. Think. And I did – I thought. I thought of how the machine's treadmill had an inbuilt springiness, a gentle bounce-back. How the chrome handles at the front of the machine were dulling slightly at the centre from years of dripped sweat. I thought about my shoes. Was I wearing the right shoes? They were the running shoes I took on tour, light running shoes with insoles and tie-fast laces, years old, but I only ever wore them for the two-week tours we did every six months. All the while, I kept thinking. Still thinking. Don't look at the TV. The door behind me opened and closed. A man discarded his towel, picked up weights, and looked at himself in the mirror. I could see what he was doing, though I tried to keep my eyes focused ahead. Chrome handles, rubber tread, TV, man watching himself in the mirror. I was getting into a stride now, the miles rolling literally on. Keep running up that hill. *Hard*. I couldn't stop myself, and glanced at the LED display. Seven minutes. I'd been running for seven minutes.

Time is not permanent or fixed, it runs according to our changing lives. Sometimes it runs slowly, sometimes quickly. Our baby son Johnny is now six months old as I write this. People who don't see him every day, every hour, people who don't hold him through the wide-awake nights or watch him working out something new every day, say 'don't they grow up quickly?'. And sometimes I reply, 'yes', to be polite, but really I think to myself – no, they don't grow up quickly. Watching Johnny grow in these few months has stretched time beyond any reasonable measure. It was the same with my daughter Maisy. Previously I'd spent years touring the world, playing concerts, recording and writing. Those years quickly shrunk into compartmentalized segments, filed and understood, a pattern of scattered, memorized chunks, huge batches of experience

188

reduced to colourful slabs of generalized diary entries. Japanese tour, 1990. Germany with Julian and Geoff. Dunst and the Greek money. The interchangeable days and nights in Woodlands Studio. America with Alabama Three, 1999. Recording Danbert's first album.

In contrast, when Maisy was born, time slowed right down. Time took its time, let me understand the enormity of life, of life-changing. Every day, a change. A new attempt at grasping. A half-formed sound. A word. Another word. Eating, crawling, toddling, walking. A succession of events that slowed down the clock, that refused to simply pass time. I resisted the urge to write everything down, to photograph every change, aware that this sudden shift in my perception of time was best kept close, savoured, and enjoyed in the moment.

Running through woods, through fields, up and down mountains, time is always relative to the changing earth. It cannot be fixed while there are a thousand elemental events to slow it down and speed it up. The highest mountain in the British Isles is Ben Nevis, its summit at 4,409 feet from its unimposing base in Achintee on the east side of Glen Nevis; unimposing, usually, in that its mountaintop is rarely visible because of the generally wet and cloudy Scottish weather. I've run up and down this mountain several times, each trip for entirely different reasons. Each time it's the same mountain, in the same place, but everything about it is different. The weather, temperature, conditions underfoot, time of day, and (most variable of them all) myself are always different. I don't want to race against myself, against my own fastest time for the ascent and descent of the mountain – in any case, it wouldn't make sense. In such an experiment there could be no 'control', since everything about the test, discounting the mountain's height, is variable. Indeed, I am not the same person from year to year, day to day or even hour to hour. There's a lovely scene in *The Simpsons* where, in a conversation with his grandpa in the old folks' home, Bart makes it clear that he wants to leave, that he's desperate to get out of there. Not that he's itching to go or anything, he says, 'but I've been here ten minutes. Which is like seven hours in kid years.'

I first ran up and down Ben Nevis when it played host to the British Championship fell race series in 1990. I completed the race route – from the Claggan Park football ground on the outskirts of Fort William and back again – in 1 hour 38 minutes. I'll never run it as fast again, and have no desire to try. I know the time because I've just looked it up on the internet, and I'll forget it by the time I reach the end of this paragraph. I next ran Ben Nevis while holidaying in the area, lured by deep snow and icy conditions. With a small sackful of provisions and extra clothing I set off not to race up the mountain but to experience it. To get to know it better, unpicking its lore and mythology, jumping across a raging Red Burn (that tells you you're halfway up), stopping at the line of the lowest clouds to get a final glimpse of the valley below, bleached by reflected light.

Racing up and down mountains (and mountain ranges) is thrilling and intense, while running them – often alone – is meditative, firing up your sense of self and place. Racing forces you to experience the enormity of a mountain (or forest, or riverbank trail) in a primal, savage rush.

Running urges you to drink it in, to explore it, to fill your head with it.

At the top of Ben Nevis are the remains of a meteorological observatory, wedges of tumbled stone to mark the place where, from 1881, scientists, geologists and geographers made daily ascents of the mountain to record conditions there. There's also a summit cairn that appears to shrink and grow depending on the intensity of the winter weather, along with a rough and ready war memorial and the guts of a piano that was left there by a team of removals men who carried it up the mountain for charity many years ago. One of the men, Mike Clark from Dundee, was quoted in a local newspaper: 'We got up to the summit plateau but it was covered in mist and was very cold. So we sat down and drank a bottle of whisky and ate a packet of McVitie's biscuits. It was very cold touching the iron frame so we built a cairn of rocks around it and left it there. The biscuit wrapper blew into the cairn and was covered up too.'

There's a shocking matter-of-factness about this wanton littering of a mountain; it's perhaps the additional details about the biscuit wrapper.

'Where's the piano gone, love? It was in the corner of the living room this morning.'

'The piano? Oh, right, that piano. Hmmm. Oh yeah, I remember now. We left it up the top of Ben Nevis.'

'You did what?!'

'Left it up on Ben Nevis, covered in a few rocks that were lying around. It's OK though, love, we threw in the biscuit wrapper too. McVitie's, they were.'

Our general dislocation from the countryside – surely a modern phenomenon – reached full expression in early

2001, when the entire British countryside was suddenly declared out of bounds. Police tape was stretched across stiles and gates; warning signs, traffic cones and newly erected fencing prohibited access to every meadow, forest, hill and valley. Everything green was a no-go area. An outbreak of foot-and-mouth disease had sent the country into a blind panic, and the government ministry responsible responded by openly slaughtering and burning huge piles of cattle carcasses. It was my fortieth year and I was forced into running sporadically and begrudgingly on the roads, seeing the trails and paths unused and overgrown. Farmers prowled around their perimeter fences daring the 'townies' to set foot inside – every road and track leading to and from farms in the Yorkshire Dales and Lake District was peppered with long, low baths of chemical cleaner; vehicles drove through the pungent, sloshing stuff and visitors – no hikers or runners! – dipped their boots. Seemingly, we were a nation under plague.

Getting off a flight to the Czech Republic to play a concert there, we were greeted at airport customs by special hand basins 'for all passengers who have travelled from Britain'. This madness (later, the general consensus was that the government had botched the whole affair, panicked into needlessly slaughtering ten million animals and closing off the countryside – and, according to a subsequent report by the Agriculture Ministry, not a single case of foot-and-mouth was attributable to a walker [or runner] during this outbreak) carried on for around nine months, the restrictions being lifted first in Scotland in the early autumn. On the day the footpaths opened around Ben Nevis, I drove for eight hours from Leeds after dark, my studded shoes and cagoule in the back. I tried to sleep in the car, but despite being exhausted from the drive I could barely sleep in anticipation of – at last – several hours of solitary mountain running. The next day I was up and onto the lower slopes of the Ben, shoes dipped in chemical cleaner and eyes lifted to the dense grey cloud. It was thick with snow up there, and the summit was invisible – this time I swung across to make a detour to Meall an t-Suidhe, a crag-strewn mountain towering over a high-level loch and – being several hundred feet lower than Ben Nevis – not quite puncturing the clouds. I wanted to catch the view before heading up into the predictable whiteout of the Ben.

Sure enough, somewhere up on the oscillating mountainside path, on the steepest part of the climb, the drizzle turned into snow and visibility dropped to a few feet. Those few feet were already white with deepening settled snow, and the greens and blues of my clothes vibrated with alien colour, out of place and strange. My feet crunched through the snow's crust, feeling at one step familiar, at the next brand new. Nan Shepherd describes how the summer's heather, though beautiful to see and smell, is best experienced underfoot, felt, trodden on. Snow is like this. There's such a childlike delight to be had from stamping a foot through unconquered snow – and more than heather, that connection between the foot and the world is for a time marked, stamped with a size-ten signature. I was here. And even up there on the flanks of Britain's highest mountain I could still leap like a happy kid into the next fresh, white step, looking back to see each imprint folding in on itself.

There's an old farmers' dictum that says, if you can't see your own footsteps behind you, it's time to take shelter. As I reached the huge, sprawling top of the mountain I knew that my safest bet was to reach the summit cairn, take a deep breath and return the way I'd come. It's easy to get lost up there, and the featureless (discounting the cairn, the ruined observatory, the war memorial and the piano. Though I've never actually seen the piano) plateau is long and broad enough to spin you into a disorientated muddle at the drop of a woolly hat. On three sides of the top of the mountain are steep cliffs dropping several hundred feet, and there are several fatalities every year. I turned around at the cairn's stone pyramid, took a compass bearing and stepped into the footsteps I'd just made, breaking into a steady run as the mountain path – known as the Pony Route – began to descend. Before long the mountain began to roll away beneath me quickly, becoming steeper, the joy of this leaping, tumbling run tempered by foreboding and common sense. Watch where you're going. Keep an eye on the compass needle. Through the spray of kicked-up snow, stay focused, pay attention. As I followed my own foot shapes down, they became weaker and weaker, as if the runner who was on his way up emerged from nowhere; this time the zigzags were ignored, and I made a long, straight, snow-broken scree run down and below the cloud line, to where the snow was wispy and sparse, the dappled white landscape getting clearer as I crossed the Red Burn and wound my way back down the mountain. Once away from the highest reaches of the Ben there's still a long and deceptively steep run back along winding paths, with boulders and loose stones lying in

194

wait. It was on this last, hurtlingly fast part of the descent that, during the Ben Nevis race all those years ago, I tripped and flew, arms spreadeagled, winding up off the track and rolling down sodden grass until I clutched myself to a stop. Mud, blood and chlorophyll. Sometimes you leave your mark on the mountain – and sometimes the mountain leaves its mark on you.

Back at the car I realized I'd been out for over four hours, and now I was sweating and tired and hungry. After a run like that there's a tangible buzz, a muscle-twitching refusal to come to such a sudden halt. Getting gloves off, untying laces, it all becomes a struggle against the easy coordination you've been enjoying. From down here Ben Nevis was still hidden – the world through a steamed-up bathroom mirror, denying you the satisfaction of looking – but I didn't need to see it now; I'd felt it, raced it, clambered up and through it. I chewed on a chocolate bar and collapsed into the passenger seat, smiling. I didn't smile to myself – I smiled to the whole, wild world.

33

The corner of New York's E116th Street and First Avenue is a blur of tenaciously anchored street furniture hastily plastered over stone, concrete and asphalt. The amount of 'street furniture' – how polite an expression for the discordant jumble of name-plate signs, warnings, instructions and enticements – at any given road and street junction is increasing. On a visit to Japan around ten years ago I looked down a side street and saw the future: nothing but brightly coloured signs at every level and on both sides, a clutter of information so extreme that the street itself disappeared beneath the weight of barked symbols and words. At 116th and First, spinning around on one axis, I see:

BIKE LANE
GEO. WASHINGTON BRIDGE
BUSES ONLY
DUNKIN' DONUTS
HAND-MADE CIGARS
1ST AVE
WESTERN UNION
ONE WAY
TENG DRAGON CHINESE RESTAURANT
99C DISCOUNT STORE

19 MILE
RFK BRIDGE
ASICS
ORBIT EAST HARLEM
LIQUORS & DELI
WILLIS AVE BR.
NAILS
RIMS
STOP

And some of it is lit, some of it old, some of it bent and broken and all of it fixed. Screwed down and riveted, edged and encased and laminated and rooted, rooted in the concrete and stone that form the walls and the floor of this single street corner of Manhattan. Imagine if, every autumn, the shop signs dried up and fell to the ground, the lampposts leaned awkwardly, the advertising hoardings withered and shrunk, the street names blew away in a storm . . .

I love the city. Not just this city in particular; I love the city with its conversation, culture and community. I love the city with its galleries and museums, its shop windows and daily newspapers, statues and cafés; its fashion and beauty and its loud, fascinating ugliness, its bars and the people in them, its taxi drivers and sewer smells and bookshops and parks. I love how a city changes because of the people in it. But it doesn't take long before I get tired in a city, tired of the combination of the ceaseless shout of the street furniture and the unyielding brutality of the architecture. These are things that don't change – or, at least, they take a long, long time to change. More time than I can afford to give them, whatever way it's measured (and my rough measurement goes like this: in terms of exhaustion, three hours running in the country, over hills, roughly equals one hour's walking around the city streets).

This buzzing, yelling corner of First Avenue today gives up its day job and hosts another drinks station, another crowd of whooping onlookers, another parade of weary, staring runners. Today this could be any New York intersection, any of the twenty-six miles, any of the 45,000 runners. Someone took a film of the race and looped it on a short cycle. Maybe it goes on forever, same determined stares, same bell-ringing, cheering crowd, same road ... the only thing that changes are the street signs. In a daydream, watching this drama repeat itself over and over again, I imagine a runner, skinny and with clenched fists, looking around as he passes. He's Sillitoe's Colin Smith, out of the juvenile detention centre now, still wearing his grey T-shirt, prison-issue shorts and flimsy shoes. He sees a sign. It says, white on a big red octagon, STOP. And he smiles, and carries on running.

34

The 2010 New York Marathon makes upwards of $25 million for its designated charities, including the American Cancer Society, UNICEF and the Children's Hospital Trust. In a world where state-funded support for healthcare and poverty relief is being withdrawn and people look to charity to help fill the gap, it seems more than just churlish of me to criticize the race, it's downright unpleasant. So 45,000 people want to pull on a pair of running shoes and donate huge amounts of money to help provide children with healthcare, clean water, nutrition and education? How could that be anything but A Good Thing? And then there's me over at the back of the smiling, waving crowd, kicking my heels and grumbling about the traffic cones and the pavement. The Christmas-stealing grouch, old Ebenezer Scrooge and me, tut-tutting as we head off up the nearest mountain to complain.

I am the killjoy, the spoilsport, the naysaying party pooper; my only defence against those who run the marathon to raise money for and awareness of children's charities (for instance) is to quietly assert that this is the best argument why the city marathon need exist. I have an instinctive admiration for people who dress up in funny costumes and run along carrying collecting buckets to raise money for hospitals: and while the CEOs, the state officials and the families of the filthy rich continue to cream off such imbalanced wealth (in the US, between 1965 and 2000, the ratio of CEO pay to that of a typical worker rose from 24:1 to 300:1), it breaks my heart to see the effort people will go to in supporting those less well off than themselves. (In Britain, while the incredible National Health Service is being systematically run down by governments – Labour and Tory alike – and sold off to private companies, nurses in uniform run through the city streets pushing beds to raise money for cancer wards and dialysis machines.)

This selfless effort and enterprise is the golden glow at the heart of the marathon's forced pageantry, the natural, saintly altruism that at best demonstrates the human leaning towards cooperation and kindliness. Yes, it's for one day only. But look – and I'll say this plainly – in the face of the woman who runs twenty-six miles to raise thousands of dollars for a hospital ward, I am truly humbled.

Look at the names of the races I could do this month in America, all within twenty miles of where I live:

Kidds 5K Race to Support the Center for Grieving Children and Their Families

Race for the Ribbon 5K for the Union Hospital Breast Health Center

Making Strides Against Breast Cancer 5K for the American Cancer Society

Elkton Christian Academy Crusader 5K Walk/Run for Salem Children's Home

Have Joy, Spread Hope 5K Run for the Joy-Hope Foundation's Mitochondrial Disease Research

200

. . . I could go on (it's a long list). Arriving in America, I was shocked at the wholesale domination of the racing scene by road-race charity-raising events; entry fees are usually upwards of $25–$40, for which there's the obligatory free shirt emblazoned with sponsors' logos and the charity being supported. Charity is big business, and has been forced to be so by the lack of compassion shown by the corporations and institutions that cream off the public wealth. The level of wealth inequality today in America – where just 1 per cent of the population own 34 per cent of the wealth – is almost double what it was in the mid-1970s. This continuing trend is replicated in Britain. In June 2010, the US Legislature passed Governor Paterson's latest budget plan, cutting another $775 million from healthcare services, bringing the total cuts to healthcare in just the last two years to more than $5 billion. In the face of this, it's little wonder that races – and the New York City Marathon in particular – are closely tied to charity funding. I don't want another outsized T-shirt, thanks – but begrudging the organizers and their chosen charities the inflated race fee is just plain anti-social. As environmental campaigner Ralph Nader put it, 'A society that has more justice is a society that needs less charity.'

The city marathon isn't without other saving graces. It acts as an introduction to running, advertises the democratic anyone-can-do-it of the sport. It's a way in, a way to begin. In a world where worsening diet and lack of physical exercise are not only making us lazy and indolent but fostering ill health and low self-esteem, the city marathon offers a relatively easy route to physical and psychological salvation. It's a goal, a recognizable target. Twenty weeks of training, one day of hurt and effort, and you've done something that your friends will respect and applaud.

And after the race is over? There's a recognized condition called 'Post-marathon Malaise'. You did it, you achieved your goal – what next? An article in *Runner's World* magazine suggests (quite seriously) 'Bring home a puppy'. It carries on, 'Or renovate your house, or book a trip to an exotic location. The point is to set an important and time-consuming non-running goal for after the marathon. This way, you'll have something to look forward to after you cross the finish line.' I've read countless other pages of advice on how to beat the post-marathon blues. Take time off, try racquetball, sleep late, spend time with your friends, plan another marathon, eat a chocolate sundae, 'Go buy yourself something. New running shoes? New watch? New car?' Nowhere have I read, 'Leave the road behind for a while. Run in a place without corporate sponsorship, cheering crowds, or bands playing bad blues music as you pass. Run back into the real world. Run for fun.' The gargantuan beast that is the city marathon doesn't want you to run away; not now. Not just when you've started. No, there's only one official solution to the post-marathon blues: start preparing for the next one. And the sponsors and organizers, like chefs adding MSG to their dishes, have you hooked.

35

I was alone. I descended from the summit of Grisedale Pike down to the wide col at Coledale Hause in the western Lake District, low cloud hanging thinly like a tatty hem. The sky was a weak, dirty-white translucence, there was drizzle in the air and I could see my breath. It was one of the year's first forays into the high mountains, a sounding out, a remembering. A winter running the relatively low Yorkshire fells often forces me to forget the tough and wearying thrill of climbing real peaks, hands-on-knees ascents and long, unwinding descents. I looked up and around and there – apparently on the steep slope of Crag Hill, in front of me and around a mile distant – was my own silhouette, huge and comical, dark and fuzzy. Around it, around this giant me waving at itself, was a circle of hazily multicoloured rings. He is risen! And has grown to about 200 feet tall! I stopped in my tracks, watching the ghost of myself, flapping and dancing alone on the mountainside opposite – a towering visual echo (no matter how involved I've become with music technology and the digital reproduction of echo and reverb, I still can't resist the urge, in tunnels and across lakes, to test the echo by shouting. *Hello –o –o –o –o!* It's the one place we can be certain of getting a resounding, affirmative answer).

There's a peak in the Harz Mountains of Germany called the Brocken that gives its name to this rare phenomenon, called a Brocken Spectre, where an observer's own shadow is cast, huge and giant-like, across the surfaces of clouds. With the sun shining from behind and under very particular atmospheric conditions, the optical illusion (for it's a trick of the eyes) can appear and disappear, blown away with the wind. Illusion or not, it's an amazing sight; a shock.

In all my years of mountain running, I'd never seen one until that moment, there on Coledale. The spectacle is one thing and the privilege of having seen it another. I could see it because I was there, in that moment, and no one else would ever see it the same way. *Look at me, the colossus with the studded shoes!* It's a sight to see, and a sight to hold in the memory, another experience to try to stuff into that cupboardful of the past that's stretching to burst its hinges now. An unexpected treat, somewhere beyond the reach of my cameraphone, a secret shared between me and a mountain ... The Spectre drifted away with the cloud and I stopped my insane flapping, and left without my dancing partner, smiling through my heavy breathing. Phew.

'Have you ever run a marathon?'

'Well, yes, but that's not important. I've seen a Brocken Spectre.'

Scottish poet Norman MacCaig's seen one, too. It's there in his poetry. MacCaig had a knack of capturing the wild beauty of a place without ever lapsing into romanticism, though his habit of smoking twenty cigarettes a day put paid to any chance of him having a go at running.

Still, ciggie stuck out at right angles to his pursed lips, he walked a stout lifetime exploring the Scottish mountains.

> *I claw that tall horizon down to this;*
> *And suddenly*
> *My shadow jumps huge miles away from me.*
> (from 'Climbing Suilven')

'Experience' is an overused (and ill-used) word. Various dictionaries give it different weights, from the weak 'a particular instance of personally encountering or undergoing something', to the more inclusive 'the totality of the cognitions given by perception; all that is perceived, understood, and remembered'. That's better. Experience is a ball-of-wax word, a sweeping word – the best way I can think to compliment it is *worldly*. Experience, moss-gathering, dream-catching, feeding off the world, guzzling it down and storing it in a belly full of life. Too often we're sold experiences as consumables, whether they be funfair rides or wax museums, movies or chocolate bars. Martin Amis's autobiography is called *Experience* and its cover shows a photograph of himself as a young boy defiantly smoking a cigarette and daring the camera to tell on him. He calls the book 'a view of the geography of a writer's mind', placing himself firmly in the hugeness of the world and everything in it. Experience, it's the stuff that shapes us, Ralph Waldo Emerson's 'Life is a series of surprises, and would not be worth taking or keeping, if it were not.' All that is perceived, understood and remembered.

'The only function that one experience can perform is to

lead into another experience.' (William James, American psychologist)

Is this true of our running? Does it lead elsewhere (somewhere, anywhere, who-knows-where), ask questions, prompt and prod and push us further? Does it offer us enough of a glimpse that we want to see more? And have you ever run a marathon? Yes, but . . .

British fell and mountain running has thrown up a bookful of characters who typify the sport, but none more so than Joss Naylor, a Lake District shepherd from Wasdale, a remote and rainswept valley in the Lake District. Joss spent the second half of the twentieth century running and racing on the fells, and stories of his exploits run from tittle-tattle to myth and on into legend (if we let them, which we will). Such was his prowess on the hills (his ability to trot up and down seemingly endless mountains at constant pace earned him not only an MBE but the general affirmation among hill runners as the sport's greatest ever athlete, and possibly its most modest gentleman, too) that in the 1970s he was offered money to compete in a twenty-four-hour endurance race at Crystal Palace in London. He went there and ran around a 400-metre track for a day and a night, clocking up 132 miles. He never did it again. Some of the fastest mountain runners have moved over to running street marathons, lured by the money; it's no surprise considering the history of hypocrisy and shamateurism surrounding organized sport. Avery Brundage, President of the International Olympic Committee from 1952 to 1972, stated that 'the devotion of the true amateur athlete is the same devotion that makes an artist starve in his garret rather than commercialise his work'. Avery

Brundage, wouldn't you guess, was a millionaire. Kenny Stuart left his Lakeland garret in 1986 having dominated mountain racing for several years (he still holds the records for both the Ben Nevis and Snowdon races) in order to win some money on the marathon circuit; he did well on the roads for three years (including a second place at the Houston Marathon in 1989) but retired because of persistent allergy problems. Billy Bland, another fell-running legend of the late twentieth century who worked as a shepherd, was very much the single-minded thoroughbred, shunning the roads and running improbably fast times around the mountain trails of Britain. His inability to transfer his fell-racing mastery to road racing is evident in the five Ben Nevis races in which he was in the lead after the descent to the foot of the mountain only to be overtaken on the final road section.

Perhaps the phrase 'single-minded' in reference to Billy is a mistake. The complex range of skills necessary for winning mountain and trail races is anything but the measured step-step-step required of road running. Visual awareness, balance, navigational sense, fearlessness, concentration, wall-climbing, river-crossing, fence-jumping, hill-climbing, scree-running, rock-scrambling – all stirred around with an essential fascination for the world under your feet. Fascination, passion, love. Wild runners will swear that this kinship with the dirt below them is something more than the simple self-worth, and sense of achievement, to be had from road running.

A recent (and very unscientific) online survey asked road runners the simple question 'Why do you run?' Well, why did they?

I have become addicted to the feeling of self-worth and clarity I get on my daily run.

I run mostly so I can eat more.

It just gives me hope to know that no matter how hard life gets, I always have the option to stand and fight.

While reading the New Testament of the Bible I kept running across the word 'endurance'. I prayed, 'Father how do you get endurance?' I looked up endurance online and 'marathons' came up. I started reading and now I'm starting to run.

It inspires disciplined habits, good posture and a confident stride. And great jeans.

When you run regularly . . . your sleeping pattern is enhanced . . . You sleep deeper.

I needed to lose weight and help myself feel better going through a divorce.

Running helps me stay sober.

I started running as a cheaper form of exercise compared to the gym.

I do it to get in better shape before football and wrestling season start.

Not a lot of fascination, passion and love there. Not a lot of fun, either. In the survey, many respondents talked of 'the runners' high' and the 'sense of achievement', but few talked in a way that would entice me to take up running – great jeans, yes, but is it actually enjoyable? Running shouldn't just be an alternative to lifting weights or avoiding cream cakes. Neither should it be a slightly less boring (and cheaper) substitute for a gymnasium treadmill. Some of the reasons given above are good reasons to run; off-road running gives you these but also throws in a

208

human-sized lucky bag's worth of surprises. Fun, play and adventure disguised as a muddied, lung-bursting test of character.

The fact is, in the woods and on the hilly paths, you can't afford to be single-minded. You simply cannot turn off, switch onto automatic, keep to a steady rhythm and pace out your miles. You can try, but you'll fall over. Bang goes the Personal Best. Single-mindedness for the city marathon runner, on the other hand, is an essential. Having established a pace, the next thing is to begin switching off the inessentials, turning out the lights as you leave each room. The world around you is unlikely to change very much in the next twenty-six miles. Pull down your cap, focus on the road six feet in front of you and tap out that cadence. Uniformity, regularity, tempo, the marathon runner's best friends. Cut out distractions, drape those cheering, well-wishing faces in a gauze of general encouragement and maybe switch on The Lovin' Spoonful to escape the present altogether.

William James's maxim 'The only function that one experience can perform is to lead into another experience' assumes that each experience somehow introduces something different, something new. The city marathons – from Boston to London, Berlin to Moscow – seem hell-bent on offering something very similar, if not the same. Same distance, obviously. Same surface, same pre-race pasta party, same sponges, same energy gels, same bands. No! Different bands! In Boston we hear a Dixieland jazz band thumping out 'When the Saints Go Marching In' at the twelve-mile mark. In London there's a Pearly King crooning 'Roll Out the Barrel' as the runners jog alongside the Thames. In

Berlin it's disco, inevitably, thump-thump-thumping in time with the squish of thousands of heavily cushioned mid-soles past the Reichstag. And in Moscow there's a blues band playing John Lee Hooker as the runners pass beneath the statue of Peter the Great. Boom, boom. But the city marathon isn't judged by its music, it's judged by the time on your watch (if the watch says it was a good marathon, it was a good marathon) or by the number of strangers who shouted 'Good job!' as you grunted through their field of vision. That's the paradox of the marathon – stuck fast in the centre of the city, and yet so divorced from the world.

36

Most people don't have the luxury of a job like mine. I can't emphasize enough how privileged I feel to be making my living by writing, playing guitar and singing. My running and racing can be slotted into all the gaps that appear in my working life in a way that would be the envy of most runners. My single stuttering defence (should I feel like I'm up for trial, along with various overpaid pop stars, for whingeing about the life of a musician) would be that my life lacks routine; and it's routine that helps runners find a training pattern and helps runners sustain fitness and form. Over the last twenty years I've snatched my running eagerly in the periods where the band isn't on tour, recording or playing weekly festivals. The lure of the summer festivals has meant that I tend to miss the bulk of the summer's running, instead spending time fighting jetlag or jogging around cities looking for parkland or woods. The absence of routine, though, is a small price to pay for the lack of regimented alarm-clock wakings, daily commutes and boredom. I'm lucky and I know it.

While living in Grassington in the Yorkshire Dales for a year in the late 1990s – in a leaning and draughty farmhouse with a family of owls and a coal-fired Aga – I found myself having to drive to a recording studio in Castleford (a distance of around fifty miles) each day for several winter months. This meant both leaving and arriving home in darkness. During that time it became clear to me how much effort many runners have to put in to train daily; worse than getting up at 7 a.m. to get ready for the drive to work is getting up before 6 a.m. to buy enough time for a run first. Or, alternatively, arriving home in the sullen charcoal of a winter's mid-evening and somehow finding the motivation to change out of work clothes and into a tracksuit before heading out to train. Both of which entail running in the dark, and thus running on roads, a daily swim against the tide of full-beam headlights.

I say this because I can see that my advocacy of off-road running, my eager celebration of mountains, trails and fields and my distaste for the city marathon, might seem like the out-of-touch bluster and bombast of the overprivileged. But around me every week at fell or trail races, and on group nights at my running club, Pudsey & Bramley, are thousands of people who, like me, have opted to run and race away from the city centres, people from every walk of life. Richard is a postman who gets up at four every morning, works a seven-hour day (plus a half-day on Saturday), sleeps for a couple of hours and then gets out onto the parks and canal banks near his home in Wortley. Brian is a technician at a hotel, works variable (and often inhospitable) hours and is out every evening along the tracks and paths of Pudsey Beck, a small but thickly wooded river that winds its way between Bradford and Leeds. Johnny works nights in a brewery, canning beers on a production line, and often turns up for races and training runs unshaven and heavy lidded, having been working all night.

It seems to me that runners will go to any lengths to feed that habit of the daily run – and, despite the darkness, off-road runners will find space and time to get away from the pavements and into the open countryside. The Leeds–Liverpool canal, a 210-mile ribbon of mucky water and dirt path twisting slowly between two of northern England's major cities, runs through some spectacular scenery, crossing the Pennines and threading together the farmland, mills and villages that defy the crushing weight of concrete-moulded progress. Every lunchtime, office workers along the entire length of the canal throw off their suits and leather-soled shoes and head for the canal's banks, escaping into this tree-lined refuge, out and away from the post-industrial grime that surrounds it. The canal gives runners (and walkers, and cyclists) the most pleasant route through, and beyond the reach of, all its towns and cities; it's an all-weather out-and-back respite from work.

I discovered during that Grassington winter that I could still squeeze some training into the day; either by setting off early and leaving time to stop somewhere along the route once the sun had risen, or by cycling the last ten or fifteen miles to the studio along the banks of the River Calder. Some off-road runners spend a lifetime discovering new ways to beat the darkness and keep their sanity, their job and their feet as far as possible off the tarmac; their reward is a daily dose of balance – the huge and open release of the outside world to pit against the enclosed and enclosing crush of work.

For some, the opportunity to run (or not run) off-road is down to more than economy of time. Sarah Rowell is a well-known figure in British running. A former international marathon runner (she finished fourteenth in the 1984 Los Angeles Olympics), she's probably more famous for her fell and mountain running, a history in itself of record-breaking and epic runs. She's also a member of my home-town running club, Pudsey & Bramley, and the author of the book *Off-Road Running* – in short, she knows a thing or two about wild running and is someone I could turn to when discussing a woman's perspective on all this gung-ho, Boy's Own-style bushwhacking.

For there's an issue here about safety, and danger, that (for various reasons) applies much more to women than to men. Despite men being far more likely to be attacked than women outside the house – various studies in the UK have it between two and eight times a greater likelihood – the threat of violent assault continues to frighten women runners into sticking to the road. The oft-published advice endlessly repeats: keep away from isolated and badly lit areas and avoid running alone. In a recent *Runner's World* magazine article, '30 Things Every Woman Should Know About Running', five of the suggestions amounted to warnings of possible attack. Bring on the fear.

Sarah Rowell's lifetime of running – of which much has been off-road – has, by her own estimate, seen her spend 70 per cent of that time alone. In total, (and in handy list form!) she has had to deal with, and I quote:

1 flasher on Leeds–Liverpool Canal
1 naked walker on Ilkley Moor in Yorkshire (we both said 'hi')
1 naked couple running in Aberdeen, Scotland

Numerous shouts of 'Zola Budd!' (yup, showing my age),
'Run, Forest, Run', and 'Get Those Knees Up!'
The occasional wolf whistle
Various kids trying to run along side me
Various owners telling me that their dog was either 'just
*   playing' or has 'never done that before . . .'*

Sarah adds:

> *There are many people, mainly women but not just, who are*
> *hesitant or even frightened about going off route – some-*
> *thing that the magazines at times play up to; 'Always run in*
> *pairs, carry a phone, tell someone where you are going . . .'*
> *But the only time in thirty years of running that I have ever*
> *felt threatened was on the promenade of a seaside town. I*
> *don't dismiss the risk, but women can do a lot to prevent any*
> *risk there is (and in terms of being attacked by men that risk*
> *is much greater in built-up areas).*
>
> *Firstly by awareness. I never run with headphones, you*
> *can't hear anything, and I have given nasty shocks to more*
> *than one woman by running past them while they were*
> *listening on their personal stereos. Secondly by attitude. My*
> *body language can't be read as 'look at me, ain't I pretty?'*
> *and I have a natural 'piss off I'm training' face!*

Most violent attacks happen in the home; mostly by relatives and acquaintances. The vast majority of those attacks
happen in the towns and cities, on the streets. The chances
of being attacked while running in the woods or hills are
minuscule – and, without being flippant, running is saving
us from that much more dangerous proven killer, *poor diet*

and physical inactivity, which are credited with over 16 per cent of all deaths in the USA. Nevertheless, pulling up the comfort blanket of statistics and ignoring the safety warnings is just dumb. Clearly, feeling safe isn't the same as being safe – just as fear of assault isn't the same as assault. I realize, too, that statistics don't offer much in the way of confidence and fearlessness.

Google 'woman runner attacked' and you'll find yourself tumbling into a series of horrific news stories that more likely than not would have you heading for the gym. Hey, it might be boring there but at least it's safe. But wait – try tapping in 'woman attacked in gym' and you'll discover another nasty bundle of violent crime. How about 'woman attacked in hospital'? Same. Try 'woman attacked in own home', and watch Google's webpage count rocket to over fourteen million results.

The house we're renting in Arden, Delaware, formerly belonged to Charlotte Shedd, an infamous communist and radical who for many years had her own radio show, broadcast weekly from a small office just off the kitchen. She was also friends with social campaigner and firebrand First Lady Eleanor Roosevelt, and I have photographs of the two of them together to prove it. Standing in our house! Mrs Roosevelt was Charlotte's daughter's godmother, and visited Arden in 1935 to talk to local artists and activists. Everyone who visits our house gets to see the photographs of Eleanor Roosevelt standing in front of the big old fireplace and surrounded by well-dressed secret service agents disguised as ordinary blokes. Eleanor Roosevelt was the first of the now commonplace 'opinionated First Ladies'. Her opinions (unlike those of, say, Barbara Bush or Nancy Reagan) resonated because she spoke out at a time when women were not expected to do so. And Eleanor, she said: *'I believe that anyone can conquer fear by doing the things they fear to do, provided they keep doing them until they get a record of successful experience behind them.'*

37

In 1990, Chumbawamba started to play a new song called 'I Never Gave Up'. The lyrics were based on words written by Primo Levi in his book *Moments of Reprieve*, an astounding memoir in which Levi (a concentration camp survivor) articulated the defiance and courage shown by many of the prisoners in Hitler's death camps. In the book, Rappoport – a camp inmate imprisoned at Auschwitz with Levi – instructs the author, should he live to see freedom, to tell the world this one thing: 'I never gave up.'

We played the song live, with its insistent chorus of 'I never gave up / I never gave up / I crawled in the mud / But I never gave up' and it immediately became a rallying cry; an emphatic singalong anthem of hope and resilience. Inadvertently it became, too, to the small group of fell runners who knew me and came to our concerts, a song about the endurance and guts of mountain runners. Of course. I crawled in the mud? Who better to understand that feeling of dragging yourself out of a clay-pit pool of sodden filth, in order to carry on, and on, and on . . . than fell runners?

This strange juxtaposition of death-camp poetics and mountain running didn't sit too awkwardly, for we knew that these runners grasped the historic significance of

Primo Levi's 'crawling in the mud'. It became a band in-joke, watching at concerts to see the fell runners making their way to the front of the hall to dance and jump around to that song. I remember a show in Manchester, announcing to a bewildered audience, that 'I'm proud to announce we have three English, one Irish, and two Scottish international athletes down the front tonight!'

Will Ramsbotham ran for Pudsey & Bramley. I first met him when he raced for a Scottish club, where we scrambled, gasped and sprinted neck and neck around the tough Carnethy 5, a mountain race on the outskirts of Edinburgh. We toppled off the last peak together and tumbled downhill to the sodden, boggy finish, a few seconds apart, covered in splattered mud. Will was a sweet and friendly bloke who somehow combined the competitiveness of fell racing with an unselfish, genial bonhomie. Sometimes I try to picture the people I know, in the instant, without deliberation – how do I picture them? Some tense, some worried, some blank-faced. Some, like Will, are smiling.

Will was one of those fell runners who'd come to Chumbawamba shows and dance like it was a training session (excellent all-round aerobic and physical workout, plenty of stretching and loosening, and often including vocal exercise). In the summer of 1993, Will travelled to Wales for a fell race and to climb. He was a keen climber, did I mention that? Climbing. The sport I always decided, right or wrong, was over the 'danger' line. Will ran the Cader Idris mountain race and won it, in a record time. The next day, he set out to rock-climb the same mountain, and, trying to untangle a rope, he fell. As he lay, fatally injured, he was cradled by a good friend who sang the song 'I Never Gave Up' to him, over and over, as they waited for the mountain rescue team.

Will's death was a shock to all of us who viewed our sport, and the mountains we climbed and crossed, as nothing more than joyous. I never sang the song on stage the same way again – it suddenly became a song for Will, despite Primo Levi's best intentions. Chumbawamba played in Edinburgh about a year later, and I was surprised and happy to see Will's former fiancée Yvette at the show. We talked and tried to laugh and got choked up about Will before the concert, and Yvette asked me a favour – could we play 'I Never Gave Up' and dedicate it to Will? 'Of course, absolutely, yes,' I st-st-stammered. I don't get nervous before concerts. Ever. Not since I first went on stage with fledgling punk band Chimp Eats Banana and couldn't work out where to plug in my guitar lead. I love to talk to people using a microphone. I see it as a privilege, something that comes with the job. It's fun. But suddenly the idea of talking about Will, to an audience, with Yvette watching and listening . . . so this is what stage fright feels like. My heartbeat sped up.

I couldn't concentrate until we got to the song. The words I thought I could say were going round and round in my head; I was rehearsing, onstage, as I sang. The time came to play the song. The concert's high-pitched clatter became a softening, wound-down drone as I introduced it. 'This is a song for my friend, Will. He died tragically, last year, in a rock-climbing accident . . . and even now I can see him in the audience, somewhere, a year ago, dancing to this song.' I don't remember what else I said. I talked for several minutes before we played 'I Never Gave Up'.

Primo Levi, survivor of Auschwitz, died in 1987. He left behind a legacy of words – thoughts, recollections and ideas bequeathed to us to help fight for something better than the world he was forced to endure. Somehow, Primo's words became, for me, a fitting way to connect the mountain runner's determination to climb to the resilience of human beings in the face of monstrous obscenity.

The 1994 Chumbawamba album *Anarchy* carried a dedication to three brilliant characters who'd recently died – Frank Zappa, Derek Jarman and Will Ramsbotham.

38

Central Park is in sight now, West 116th Street meeting Fifth Avenue at a point where the spectators – some of whom have been standing here for several hours, scanning the masses of running bodies for a face they'll recognize – are running out of steam. They ring their bells more than they yell, wave their flags and banners more than they whoop. The coloured sludge of runners has developed limps, hobbles and wobbles. It sways and slows, sometimes walks, picks up steam and begins to run again. I waver between a gut-felt admiration for each and every one of them and a genuine incomprehension. I once watched a schoolboy bang his head repeatedly on a school desk like a slow and demented woodpecker, thud thud thud – back then it was some kind of demonstration of fear and panic, someone trapped and scared. Here that same headbanging monotony is a privilege, it costs hundreds of dollars, takes months of training to perfect. It looks like it achieves about the same qualitative result. This really is a race where the journey comes a very poor second to the destination; the finishing makes up for the doing.

The words I use throughout this book to try to describe my sense of wonder when I'm out running on the moors and mountains – adventure, beauty, change, mystery – these words are alien here. In a café off Third Avenue a woman checks her iPhone. She's tracking her boyfriend's progress in the race via an electronic chip tied to his shoelace.

'He's running 9.48 minute mile pace,' she says to her friend.

'Oh. Is that good?'

'I don't know.'

39

New York City is an astounding place. It startles and bewilders me every time I visit, and I love it. I love its peculiarities, its sense of character. I love the pizza there – best pizza outside Italy, without a doubt – the people, the galleries, the diners. The bars with their doors open, heavy wooden stools, glasses full of ice (how un-English), signed photographs of baseball players and film stars. The Strand bookstore on Broadway, shelves and shelves full of second-hand words, well-read words, all those spines jam-packed and wedged together, quiet and hushed among the noise and blare of the street outside (and a great place for an adventure). Central Park, all done up fancy for winter, the ice rink where people skate beautifully and nonchalantly at the same time, because any other way wouldn't fit with the city – it isn't a shouty, look-at-me-I'm-wonderful city like LA or Rome; it's a city that knows it's wonderful without having to shout.

New Year's Day, 1995. It was my birthday, it was snowing and I was here with Casey, who's a photographer. She had an appointment to photograph someone over in Brooklyn, so she left me to my own devices for a day. I imagined myself as Guy Debord, drifting for a while, clueless and wonderfully directionless, watching the snow pile up in thick wedges against the shop fronts and in the parks. Snow grew around the rims and along the netting of the basketball hoops. People braced themselves against it, sheltered from it, dashed into cafés to get away from it. Cars moved more slowly and my walk turned into a trudge. I loved it, of course, this walking with nowhere to go, takeaway hot chocolate and Burnley football scarf, watching the city's turmoil and muddle in a fight to the death with the drifts and puddles. I was an outsider drinking in a place so chock-full of mythology that it's hard to make sense of it as a place where people get up, go to work and go home like everywhere else.

I passed a cinema and looked to see what was showing: a new film by Ken Loach, British director of countless gritty, socially conscious films and famously the man who made *Kes*, the archetypal 1960s British working-class film. I read the accompanying blurb and looked at the stills. *Ladybird, Ladybird,* starring Crissy Rock. Winner, 1994 Berlin Film Festival International Critics Award. 'There is probably not an actress in Hollywood who could come within ten miles of this performance.' I went in. It's my birthday, and I'll do what I want to. Two hours later I came out, the snow was two hours deeper and I was crying. I'd just watched the most unrelentingly tragic movie ever made. Ken Loach doesn't always do happy endings, and this time he decidedly didn't. (Not to give the film's main theme away, but – is there anything sadder than watching a woman having her children taken away from her?) So I stood there wiping my eyes with the back of a glove, the glare of daylight on New York's snow not helping. I carried on walking, wandering, following some notion of romantic tourism, only this time with blurry eyes. And then I started to laugh, because I knew I was in my own tragic-comic film, and that's what can happen in New York – it's a place where you get to appear in a more interesting version of your own life.

There was the time in 1998, the band and me in a bar across from the Mercury Lounge, where we'd been playing. By rights, New York should be the same for us as it's always been – we love it here, whether we're playing top of the bill in a two-thirds full CBGB's or a packed Madison Square Garden supporting Aerosmith – but in the post-'Tubthumping' topsy-turvyness we'd been invited to a bar where record company executives bought us drinks and introduced us to people who wanted to meet bands who'd had a hit record. It was a sports bar, and the walls were decorated with autographed baseball bats and basketball shirts and multicoloured pennants. And while we were in there, the representative from Universal Records told us that there were some guys who would like to come and say hello, they'd just finished a game and they loved our record and in fact the song plays every time they go out into the stadium, and they're obviously a famous team, judging by the commotion – and suddenly the room was filled with huge bears disguised as blokes, necks as big as truck wheels and foreheads that blocked out the light. They were as wide as they were tall, and they lined up politely to shake our hands, our feeble guitar-playing hands clasped by those five-fingered mechanical diggers. They smiled and laughed and joked with us and then disappeared, and it was only when they'd gone that we realized how easily they'd filled that whole bar with the heavy smack of athleticism, a wholesome, pumped-up, insanely power-ful six-man handshake.

Dunst looked at me and arched his eyebrows. Leant forward and whispered, 'Who were they?' And I whispered back, 'I've no idea. Should we have known?' And eventually the other people in the bar started to talk again and we discovered that these men were the New York Rangers, the city's ice hockey team, and that they really wanted to meet the people who sang the song they'd been playing hockey to. I imagined their disappointment – eight skinny white English musicians in a bar who shook hands like they were waving royal handkerchiefs. And what struck me was the magnificent blast of energy and vigour they'd carried with them – that's what happens when you're at the very top of your sport, I thought to myself. And I remember seeing two Leeds United foot-ballers in a shop in Leeds city centre and thinking the same thing – these super-athletes, those who dedicate their lives to sport, who train and work out every day, they crackle and spark with machine-like, thoroughbred, compressed potential.

And I think of the top wild runners I've seen up close; some of them I know. Fell runners, mountain runners and trail runners. Those who win world mountain running championships, who break long-distance records, who ascend and descend mountains faster than the rest of us; and you know what? They're some of them tall, some of them short. They're skinny, or well-built, or round-shoul-dered; they're bow-legged or long-legged or knock-kneed; they're not machines at all. Ian Holmes, British champion fell runner for several years in the early 2000s, strains to reach 5 ft 7 in in height, and runs in quick pit-pat-pit-pat steps as if dancing on his toes. Rob Jebb is Holmes' running partner at Bingley Harriers and a cyclo-cross, mountain racing and world sky running champion. He's 6 ft 2 in, wiry and ungainly, limbs swinging awkwardly. Sometimes the pair race together, and it's like watching a comedy double act.

Looking at the leaders in the New York City Marathon, watching them cruise past in that first group of ten or twelve runners, I see a general body shape; there are a few inches of difference here and there, but essentially there's a well-tuned, perfectly developed shape and size for top marathon running. An ideal ratio of sinew, bone, muscle and fat that works best, and towards which these runners will gradually gravitate. Of course. This is a single-surface sport played out time and time again in the same way. If you're to be a top hockey player – then you'd better be well-built, tough, tall, and have hands that can smother someone's entire head. If you're running city marathons – be average height, lean and muscular. And if you just want to run for fun, after a night out in New York? Be any shape you like.

The first time I came here, in 1982, I was walking with friends down a street in uptown Manhattan in the early hours of the morning when we saw a group of four or five African–American guys on the corner in front of us. As we paced uneasily towards them, they shuffled and looked up, forming a semi-circle. *Uh-oh*, we thought, *we've had it now*. Within twelve or fifteen feet, we were still trying to decide whether to run or not when that gang of boys suddenly burst into song – a cappella harmony singing,

228

real New York doo-wop. It was one of the most enchanting sounds I'd ever heard. It wasn't just beautiful; it also challenged my fear of the city, challenged my small-town prejudices, and made me aware of the possibilities of a big, mixed-up, multicultural community. I decided there and then that I loved this city. I still love New York, whatever I might think about its marathon.

New York is a city built for living, for entertainment, for eating out, for discovering bars and shops you didn't know existed, for sitting in parks and watching the world go by, a city built to accommodate everyone from the Bronx to Central Park South, from Madison Square Garden to CBGB's, from Frank Sinatra to The Ramones. It's a place of extremes, a place that somehow overcame the cruel irony of Ellis Island and the Statue of Liberty (where the huge green goddess said 'Welcome' while a man in an office stamped 'Refused Entry' on your identification papers) to become so cosmopolitan and diverse that it was one of the first places to which the term 'melting pot' was applied (in 1845, Ralph Waldo Emerson, controversially for the time, welcomed the idea of a culturally and racially mixed 'smelting pot'). Nearly 170 languages are spoken here; 36 per cent of the city's population is foreign-born. It's not Burnley, Lancashire, that's for sure.

It's hard to fault the history (and the ensuing mythology) of New York – significantly, for me at least, it's the home, past or present, of Alan Ginsberg, Diane Arbus, George Gershwin, Patti Smith, Emma Goldman, Lenny Bruce, Andy Warhol and The Talking Heads (to name a few). Its landmarks hum and its people, in turn, hum along – New Yorkers love their city, and given half a chance they'll tell you this. The diversity means there's something for everyone; turn a corner and you can be in a different world. And in a city with such a mix of ancestry, immigration and heritage, no one cares where you're from.

And yet – and yet . . . New York is not a place to run 26.2 miles. It's a place to make music, to dance, to paint and act and sing, to drive a taxi and shout shout shout as you drive, to cry to yourself in the snow, to eat what you like (and when you like), to spray-paint a eulogy to Joe Strummer on a wall, to sleep in a park, shivering under newspapers and cardboard, to sleep in a five-star penthouse overlooking Central Park, to write, compose, work, sleep – anything but run a marathon. Yes, this city loves to watch a marathon. But is that reason enough for 45,000 people to run one?

40

Driving up the winding valley from Oakhurst, California, and into Yosemite National Park, I click up and down through radio stations alternating classic rock, country music and religious sermons. Away from the cities, American radio seems to regress into a world of conservatism and fixed tradition which seems so out of step with the history and legacy of Yosemite: one of the very first environmentally protected areas of natural wildlife and habitat in America, the birthplace of the environmental movement, an area of constant change, adventure and openness.

John Muir's contribution to that movement can't be underestimated. Through a lifetime of wanderings and scramblings, he graduated from a man who was out to discover the relationship between himself and the earth into an activist who reluctantly uncovered the relationship between the earth and the politics which could either destroy or save it.

Seeing the aftermath of the rush to colonize the West – which left in its wake hundreds of abandoned towns and mines, dubious claims on huge acreages and a policy of aggressive herding and deforestation – Muir was one of the first people to understand the dangers of plundering the earth of its resources without caring about the consequences. He wasn't radical by nature; his love of the mountains, of the valleys and pastures and trees, made him a radical.

Reaching Yosemite in a winding snake of vehicles I'm reminded of John Muir's distaste of tourism, knowing full well that I'm part of that tourist onslaught. See how we drive in our vehicles, pay our $20 entry fee, slow down to gaze at the wonder that is Yosemite Valley. Look at us, disgorging from our cars, coaches and campers, cameras on tripods, sandwiches packed, soft drinks cooled.

It's late May and there's a sense of summer approaching – everyone's eager to wear short-sleeve shirts and summer dresses, and shopkeepers are returning to reopen stores left freezing and alone through the winter. But despite today's clear blue skies, from down here it looks like there's deep snow on the upper reaches of the crags and slopes. Winter hasn't retreated just yet.

But oh, what a sight Yosemite Valley is. It's shockingly, incredibly beautiful – mountain walls rising sheer and vertical from the valley floor, improbably huge. People gather in groups around the same vantage points, pointing and clicking excitedly. We stand in awe of something truly extraordinary; something that no amount of Ansel Adams photographs could properly capture. They say there's the one word a writer should never use:

indescribable.

But right now, writing this, I wonder whether even John Muir's thrilling and excitable prose ever caught the utter grandness of this spectacle. Perhaps the best thing his writing does, for me, is to prompt me to visit and see for myself, to travel across a continent in order to run along those gnarled and meandering mountain ledges and sky-high forest tracks. And despite the congregation of tele-photo lenses, queues for the toilets and hot flasks of coffee, I suspect that an hour of running will shake off this massed valley-bottom throng and leave me alone – up there – to look properly at these giant, living slabs of rock, at the water that drives through its cracks and fissures and hurls itself off and into the space between cloud and sky. Indescribable, yes. The one thing a John Muir or an Ansel Adams can't capture is the psychogeography of a place, the way that place changes because I am in it, feeling it, touch-ing it, altering it with every shift of my gaze, with every step. To feel the loose rock below my running shoes and to connect it to the awesome grandeur of Yosemite is to begin to sense one's place in the world. Not to feel small and worthless – far from it – but to feel like an essential part of this landscape. Running here – like running through the post-Industrial Revolution ruins of northern England – is to run through history.

I lace up my shoes, pack a small backpack with food, water and emergency clothing, and set off. The first few miles, following the path up to the spectacular Yosemite Falls, is an effort of weaving in and out and around the school parties and excursions. Tripping lightly up the well-maintained but steep and craggy path, I'm shocked to see some of the day-hikers wearing only flip-flops. I suspect they'll be hoping there's a restaurant at the top. Towards the top of the tourist trail there are incredible views of Upper Yosemite Falls, a plunging, deafening roar of a river hurling itself from the roof of the mountain in a crashing, screaming suicide:

Aaaaaaaaaaaaaaaaaaaaaaaaaaaaaaaaaagggggggghhhhh.

This is a waterfall that looks like it isn't made of water. Physically, the white stuff hurtling 1,500 feet to its crashing resurrection has the image of thick, thrown, chalk dust or powder; only the light drizzle of spray from 400 yards away lets you know that stuff is wet. It reminds me, strangely, of school – Burnley Grammar School, a maths teacher called Mr Saunders. His principle method of instruction seemed to be throwing the wooden-handled chalk duster at boys' heads. Just as your thoughts were starting to wander down the path from school and across to the girls' high school, their hockey fields all green and lush . . . bang! You were hit on the head by a chalk duster, the cloud of chalky fallout mushrooming and settling. Did it help me to learn mathematics? Of course not.

At the top of the falls, the day-walkers turn around and head back down. This is where all those years of wild running become useful – to be able to carry on, off the beaten track, away from the picnicking hordes, off to something, somewhere. It's so snobbish, this trail running. As if by wearing studded shoes and shorts we enter some kind of hiking aristocracy; that's rubbish, obviously. But what we do by devoting our time to running in the wild is give ourselves the chance to go further – the chance to escape the well worn for the barely trodden.

The sun is at its height and I'm up, up and away beyond the guidebooks' staple view of Upper Yosemite Falls. Even this far into the year, the snow is still on the ground up here, lots of it. As I climb away from the falls and towards Eagle Point, the snow gets thicker. Suddenly, footprints disappear. There is no trail. Only snow, scattered forest and my map and compass. It's almost cartoonish, the snow – so perfect, smoothed and rounded into icing sugar mounds, at the same time both near and far away, crystal sparkles playing tricks with my eyes. Blink. Clouds of my own breath trying to fuzz up the intense clarity of the pine needles, the tree bark, my gloved hands scooping air as I run up, up, up.

As the snow deepens, the run becomes a trudge becomes an adventure (weaving in and out of the forest and heading up towards Eagle Point, across briefly exposed boulders and precarious wind-sculpted snowdrifts) and by turns becomes a danger. The snow thickens to a pathless, blanketed white anonymity. Exciting! I follow compass bearings to the top of the mountain. The stillness is incredible. Nothing. No, wait – snow falling in a clump from a tree. Creaking. Tapping, somewhere. And then, again, nothing. This is a place to shout poetry into. I do. There's a line of John Muir's writings that I love, that I remember:

The power of imagination makes us infinite.
THE POWER OF IMAGINATION MAKES US INFINITE!

D'you hear me?!
THE POWER OF IMAGINATION MAKES US INFINITE!

And then I turn around and head back down, scrunching through the two-foot-deep snowdrifts, retracing my own lonely footprints, elated and fulfilled. Skipping down, down, joining the tourist path and saying my 'thank yous' past every walker, I wonder about a life without running. Without having that thing – wild running – that takes me

235

beyond the top of the tourist path and into the unknown. And I think: I've seen what it's like to be able to go up, far above the waterfall, onto the skyline, looking out over the valley from above. I've seen it, glimpsed the view from higher up, and now I can't go back.

The next day I return and run, climb and clamber up the opposite side of the valley. Every waterfall, every summit, every snatched view down plunging valleys and up to grandiose mountaintops, makes the running less important – it becomes a way to experience, a way to look and breathe all this in.

Afterwards I drive south down the valley, away from Yosemite, and listen to a radio station where a preacher is teaching a lesson. It's entitled, 'Leading The Way', the good pastor instructing me that there is a 'Gift of Giving' that involves prayers, confession and pledging money to his Leading The Way Ministry, at a PO box in Atlanta, Georgia. There's a DVD of his talks on the Gift of Giving, and it costs $55. Meanwhile, two digital clicks further down, a Christian talk show is discussing the forecasted Rapture and subsequent End of the World which has been prophesied to begin this Saturday at 6 a.m. Pacific Standard Time, commencing with a huge earthquake right here in California.

Which gets me thinking about John Muir and the mountains, about running, nature and spirituality. During his time in the wild, over years of watching the earth and seeing how it lived and breathed, mutated and regenerated, Muir shifted from a position of Creationism to being a follower of the (newfangled!) Darwinian idea of evolution, and a personal understanding that God is in all

Nature: an idea called *pantheism*. A belief that God – or whatever you want to call your God – is all around us, in the world and in the trees, rivers and mountains. Exchange the word 'God' for 'Nature' and you begin to reach an understanding of this all-encompassing divinity; wind, rain, animals, humans, earth, sky . . .

Several years ago I joined a good friend of mine, John Jones, on a walking tour. John is a folk singer with Oysterband, a stalwart of the English folk music scene, and he was recording a new album and preparing to play concerts to promote it. But – he'd had an idea. He wouldn't just play concerts in various towns and cities around England. He would instead string together a series of dates that might be joined together by walking. He would, together with whoever might be playing with him, walk from venue to venue, always across country.

I met up with John in his home town, Titley, towards the end of May, in a farmhouse tucked away on the English–Welsh border, and after an afternoon's rehearsal and an evening at the local pub, we set off the following morning on John's strange and wonderful adventure, tramping over rough ground, rippling hills and beaten paths – up to twenty miles a day – before setting up, soundchecking and playing, wearing the red faces of sunned, weathered walkers. John holds dearly to pantheism, and each night on stage he would describe what he felt was the day's most pantheistic moment. Seeing birds of prey swoop over woods, watching long grass blowing in rhythmic waves. Pantheists don't believe in a personal god, or of a creator god; only in a universal, all-encompassing unity in which nature is the centre. This is how John explained it as we walked up

Hergest Ridge (a hill I knew previously only as the title of an album by Mike Oldfield), his spiritual gravity interlaced with ridiculous tales of growing up in small-town Yorkshire, where teen culture seemed to be based on dancing, fighting, drinking and sex.

'Ere, pal – were you looking at my bird?'

'No, mate – just watching the grass blowing in rhythmic waves.'

Richard Dawkins, in his book *The God Delusion,* did pantheism no favours by describing it as 'sexed-up atheism' (it isn't). Famous pantheists include Albert Einstein, D. H. Lawrence, Emerson, Thoreau, Lao-tzu and Walt Whitman. And I picture them together, there on the windswept crown of Eagle Point in Yosemite, smiling for the camera against a backdrop of the magnificent Half Dome, rearing watchfully over the Yosemite Valley.

41

Norman Walsh began his working life as an apprentice at Foster's shoe manufacturers in Bolton. The Second World War had just ended and before long Norman was made responsible for producing shoes for professional athletes. For the 1948 Olympic Games (held in London), he made shoes for most of the British Olympic team. He went on to set up his own company in 1961, taking over part of his dad's repair shop to construct and sell his exclusively fashioned sports footwear, working up to eighty hours a week. His main customers were for many years rugby players, but gradually Norman's glove-like running shoes (often spiked), made of incredibly light leather uppers and without a mid-sole, became the mainstay of his work.

During the 1970s Norman Walsh met up with English Lake District fell runner Pete Bland and developed a shoe specifically for trail and mountain running. Again, a feature of the shoes – which were improved, but not drastically remodelled during the following three decades – was the absence of a cushioned mid-sole, and very little ankle support; it was felt that hill runners needed to feel the grass, mud and rock beneath them in order to increase traction, and were also required not to cushion their ankles but to allow the ankle to become strong by its natural movement over varied ground.

Around the same time, over at the University of Oregon, Bill Bowerman and Phil Knight were creating the first Nike shoe, the Cortez – named after the Spanish conquistador who notoriously massacred and plundered his way through Central America. The Cortez was different from existing running shoes in that it had an enlarged mid-sole at its heel, encouraging heel-strike running and made specifically to capitalize on Bowerman's own creation of the 'jogging' craze. The shoe started a trend that would continue into the present, with recent reports of Nike having a $17 billion annual turnover.

The Walsh shoe quickly became the footwear of choice for hill and off-road runners in Britain, sticking to the initial design principles that gave rise to its reputation as 'a mountain-racing slipper'. My first pair of Walsh shoes, bought sometime around the end of the 1980s, were so completely out-of-the-box comfortable (compared to the huge, squashy Hi-Tec Silver Shadows I'd been bouncing around in) that I immediately came to an understanding of the way our feet are supposed to work efficiently and safely over rough ground. My ankles got stronger, I ran more on the front of the foot instead of the heel, and I could 'feel' the way the earth shifted its shape, hardness and angle with every step. In the vernacular, nature doesn't do pavement.

It took almost a quarter of a century before the running world began to catch up with the idea of the 'minimalist shoe'. Walsh had simply carried on producing the same basic, suitable product that Norman and Pete Bland had come up with all those years ago, while the ever-expanding running shoe behemoths up in the big cities were inventing thousands upon thousands of variations of what we can now call 'the big squashy brick'. Then, in 2009, a book by Christopher McDougall – *Born to Run* – went public with its call for runners to think again about the shoes they were wearing. A book primarily about the author's attempt to run a fifty-mile race in the heart of Mexico's Copper Canyons and his investigation of the legendary Tarahumara people who practise minimal (light sandals!) and barefoot running, McDougall unwittingly spawned a revolution in running footwear. The open secret that was running without those big squashy bricks went public, and first runners themselves (especially those prone to years of road-running-shoe-induced injury) followed swiftly by the shoe manufacturers jumped in with both feet. Yes, including Nike, with their 'reduced running' shoes with suitably bandwagon-trailing names (the Free Run, indeed).

One advantage of all this growth in minimal running shoe design is that people like me, who've spent years avoiding stack-heeled ultra-supportive white mesh monsters, now have a range of shoes to choose from. Like many British fell runners, I still believe that the Walsh shoe – with its soft-rubber spiked sole, hardly altered from the original mid-1970s design – is the most comfortable, practical and fit-for-purpose off-road shoe, but then I'm attracted as much to the tradition and history of the initial radical design as to shoes boasting annually updated market-driven colours and models. In the USA, the barefoot runners (and their allies, the natural, low-to-the-ground, minimalist

241

masses, gathering behind them) are madly evangelical about their choice of (or refusal of) footwear. There's a feeling that they may have been sold a lie for decades, a lie whose cost can be counted in inflamed Achilles tendons, chondromalacia (runner's knee), iliotibial band syndrome (good name for an indie rock group), plantar fasciitis (inflamed heels) and (last but not least, in a highly respectable fifth place) shin splints.

It's easy to see how we failed to spot this earlier; the all-encompassing power and reach of the sportswear manufacturers is almost absolute, and their very size (Nike are the running shoe brand leader in 160 countries) makes it hard to see the alternatives. Anyone who knows anything about English football can see the power vacuum created by the multi-billionaire teams, and how the small-town clubs surrounding these mega-corporate teams have to watch in vain as local young kids beg their parents to buy them replica Manchester Utd and Chelsea shirts instead of supporting their local club.

For a while the CEOs of major running shoe companies simply dug their huge squashy heels in, crying 'foul!' – but the little boy had pointed the finger at the king, and, yes, he was definitely naked (or at least minimally shod). One company chairman chose to throw McDougall's book title back at him, writing, 'We were all born to run. But the ultimate goal, of course, is to keep running for the long haul.' Which is strange, considering the overwhelming evidence that wearing minimal footwear leads to fewer injuries. I gave up running on pavements and roads more than a decade ago, after one too many winters nursing inflamed knees and aching shins. Since then I've run almost every day with only the wear and tear of wild running to show for it; and all the cuts, scratches and gashes – along with the inevitable stiffness following a 3,000-foot descent and the odd black toenail – don't count. They're just markers on a path, notes in a diary. A record of the literal highs and lows, the hard and the soft, the flat and the steep. Experience written on the body, as Jeanette Winterson puts it: *'The accumulations of a lifetime gather there.'*

42

Strangely, the chorus of the one song for which most people remember Chumbawamba might slot in neatly as a subheading: *Run Wild: I Get Knocked Down, But I Get Up Again.* I don't know how it happened, 'Tubthumping' and its success, other than to affirm that it wasn't just a happy accident. I can honestly say it was fifteen years in the making – a collection of circumstances that can best be summed up by the lovely quote, 'luck is a matter of preparation meeting opportunity' (Oprah Winfrey said that, and it's the second and last time I'll quote her in this book, despite relishing the role of matchmaker to strange bedfellows. Oprah, meet Thoreau).

The older I get, the more I realize that my ability to run up, down and through whatever wild terrain I can find isn't just the natural, easy run-in-the-park that I once thought. At fifty years old I want to assume I've got half a century still to come; only this second half will take more effort. I see people around me getting fat, losing their hair, making low, quiet 'ohhhhh' and 'ahhhhh' sounds whenever they get up from a chair. Clearly, the getting up again gets harder. I can see myself in a few decades playing concerts at the old folks' home: 'I get knocked down, and with the help of a sturdily built carer and a steady diet of vitamin and iron tablets, I get up again.'

Motivational books inform me that they key to 'getting up again' is all about self-discipline and determination – true, but that's not enough for me. Heading off into a West Yorkshire drizzle of a day, forsaking family, wood-burning stove and laptop for an hour along the sodden fields and hedgerows around Pudsey Beck, I need more than discipline, I need fun and enjoyment. I need to love those fields, every squelch. I don't want my running to feel grey as pavement, hard as asphalt, repetitive as a flashing LED on an expensive watch. I want whatever the weather can chuck at me, I want my running to slap me across the face and wake me up.

The old Irishman in the song, who falls over in the street singing 'Oh Danny Boy . . .', he gets up because he loves life. In Aristotle's *Rhetoric*, the philosopher concluded that 'every action must be due to one or other of seven causes: chance, nature, compulsion, habit, reasoning, anger, or appetite'. Of these seven, I can safely disregard six as just not convincing enough reasons to get me out of the house in a pair of shorts. I don't want my running to be anything other than the last of his reasons – *appetite*. In other words, desire. Freud later referred to it as the 'Pleasure Principle', the hunger for joy.

Running forest paths and mountain trails – watching the world around me and beneath my feet change, daily – elevates exercise to pleasure and makes hard work fun. So much fun that sometimes it's just play! Sliding down snowy slopes, clambering up rocky outcrops, catching tree branches to swing around corners . . . it's the stuff we did as kids. The joy of life in the exercise of one's energies. Perfect. Yes, I have no intention of stopping – and I somehow can't see myself in that care home singing 'Tubthumping'. Because as long as my running is fun – and with a world full of trails and hills to explore, there's no reason it should stop being fun – then I'll carry on. I'll get slower. I'll fall down more. But as it says in the song, I'll get up again, muttering under my breath something about Oprah Winfrey and Henry David Thoreau.

43

Our connection to the earth – our physical attachment to it, and our personal experience of it – is diminishing by degrees. Walking is continuing to decline. In Britain, between 1986 and 2005, the average proportion of journeys made on foot fell from 34 to 23 per cent, from over a third to under a quarter. The total distance walked by each person, each year, fell from 244 miles in 1986 to around 200 miles in 1995. These figures don't specify countryside walking; in fact, the most popular reason for walking in Britain is *to go shopping*.

There's a golf course in Pudsey, several runnable miles from where I live in Armley, skirted by a footpath that links several woodland trails. The golf course is bound at one side by a small river – Pudsey Beck – a twisting, rushing thing barely wide enough to warrant footbridges but, after rainfall, shouty enough to warn you away from its edge. For the past two years, in the deepest part of the river, there's been a single upturned shopping trolley, wheels and underbelly breaking the surface, a twenty-first-century carcass that doesn't seem to rot or rust. This is the world, in one snatched visual image: all the singing harmony of a fast-flowing river interrupted by a stranded, abandoned trolley.

'Want to know how green your local Tesco is? Our green tours now mean you can go behind the scenes and see the environmentally friendly features of your store.'

Now there's a good day out. One consequence of our physical disconnection from the world outside our urban environments is that, despite incredible technology that can effectively create networks and forge communities across the globe, we're disengaging from the reality (and that's not the cameraphone/laptop screen reality) of our gradual destruction of the planet. We're beginning to detach ourselves from the stink, buzz and downpour of the countryside, replacing it with concern over how best to recycle plastic bags.

For most of us, environmental ruin – seemingly measured in our commitment to energy-saving light bulbs – comes from a place of theory and research; it barely affects us personally. Schoolchildren learn about how greenhouse gases are 'bad for the planet' while not having much sense of what 'the planet' outside the towns and cities actually looks, sounds or feels like.

Additionally, the language of the environmental movement has been hugged half to death by the very companies and politicians spearheading global chaos. After the Deepwater Horizon disaster of 2010, the largest marine oil spill in history, I can only wonder how the fishing communities along the coast of Louisiana (and further afield) viewed BP's well-advertised commitment to the environment, with its oft-repeated support of 'clean fuels technology' and 'renewable energy resources'.

'Blood samples from eight individuals from Florida and Alabama, male and female, residents and BP cleanup

workers were analyzed for volatile solvents. The blood of all three females and five males had chemicals that are found in the BP crude oil.' (Report from the Waterkeeper Alliance)

In 2009, BP became the New York City Marathon's 'official fuel', sponsoring it in an attempt to draw on 'the links to energy and performance between running and automobiles'. BP is one of the 2012 London Olympics' biggest sponsors, with a deal valued at $58 million. Sebastian Coe, the Games' organizing committee chairman and former world record middle-distance runner, said, in response to questions about the sponsorship following the oil spill, 'The partnership is still really strong. BP's track record is one of the best. They understand the movement behind the games.'

That is, a movement under the protection of the International Olympic Committee, or what *The Progressive* magazine critically refers to as 'that sewing circle of monarchists, extortionists, and absolved fascists'. The Olympics – while being a showcase for some of the best athletes in the world – is primarily a rolling advertisement for corporate sponsors, financial movers and political shakers. The 'movement' was long since dislocated from its own blandly worded code of ethics, just as we accept the gradual disassociation of organized sport from its simple origins.

Webster's defines the noun 'sport' as an 'activity engaged in for relaxation and amusement'. And that's what wild running in part attempts to do: celebrate sport as 'amusement'. Fun. A sport not peppered with petro-chemical logos, not fronted by smiling politicians. A sport that roots itself not in profit and power but in the earth. There are times when I stop during a run – not a get-my-breath-back stop but a lungs-full-gulping-it-all-in stop – just to measure my place in the landscape. The hugeness of it all, and how I'm a part of it, my mucky legs connecting to the ground as if they were shoots growing up from it. Nan Shepherd calls it 'walking the flesh transparent', becoming truly part of your surroundings, body and earth one big jumble of life. Running through this experience fuels both my cynicism of organized, big-money sport and my joy and delight in the simplest, most natural of pleasures. (Watching Johnny explore the vast carpeted world of the living room, sitting backstage singing unaccompanied harmony with people whose voices I know and trust, jumping up to celebrate a goal . . .) Daily running through parks, woods, fields, forests and mountains means a regular dose of that natural pleasure, and in turn deepens my anger when I read of oil spills, displaced communities, war-wearied countries and people starving as a result of the efficiently grinding wheels of modern economics. There's the point of all this, in its own neat advertising slogan: get a regular dose of natural pleasure.

There's a hillside monument perched high above Yorkshire's Calder Valley, a great grey stone obelisk named Stoodley Pike. Built originally to commemorate the end of the Napoleonic Wars, it was struck by lightning and destroyed in 1854. Two years later and at the end of the Crimean War it was rebuilt (according to the inscription at its base) 'WHEN PEACE WAS RESTORED'. A monument not to victory, but to peace. It stands around 130 feet high, beautiful in its dark, heaving presence, keeping a peaceable eye on the rough, rolling moorland

and seascape like an oversized buoy. The hills around the Calder Valley are scattered with boulders, former giants' marbles, and even in mid-summer this rough, grassy landscape can be as windswept as an ocean.

I slept inside the monument once, running through dusk, into nightfall and bedding down in a corner of its dark innards. It's never quiet there. The elements are always whooshing and whistling around the monument, and on calmer days the sheep gather there to gossip. Despite running to, from and around Stoodley Pike a million times (or a trillion, or more) it still fascinates me, a touchstone (literally) in so many long and circuitous moorland runs. I set out on a recent run up to the Pike from the valley below, just as the sun was beginning to disappear, knowing it was a full moon and hoping for a cloudless night. Sure enough, within an hour of a panting, wheezing climb, and cresting a horizon, the moon appeared as a gigantic orange disc, hovering grandly above a moortop forest. A Max Ernst painting, the daubed orange huge and watchful.

I was wearing a headtorch, a shining pool of light jogging along in front of me, and as the moon rose, so the torch's light became less and less relevant. I approached the Pike, switched off my own puny light and turned to place the monument edge as a silhouette against the moon. Ridiculously, it's at times like this that I swear: I rarely swear, but here was a time and space to throw words to shock myself. Words that say, '!', words that express nothing but exclamation.

There's an expression: 'Replace fear of the unknown with curiosity'. It reminds me of baby Johnny grasping for anything and everything, reminds me of my own adolescence, of the lives of my heroes, of Enlightenment scientists, of explorers, wanderers, thinkers – and of so many runs that have taken me into places outside the world I was accustomed to. Me and my running shoes, dwarfed by this hand-built Yorkshire stone towering above me, and lit up by a huge and whitening moon.

I love the word 'curious'. Love how it looks, with its upright, straightbacked 'i' surrounded on both sides by curling, circling letters, as if they're all whispering their playful wonderings and questionings into the rigid i's ears. Anyone who knows cats will understand the nonsense of the expression 'curiosity killed the cat'. Cats are little else but furry balls of curiosity. It may be more accurate to say Henry Ford killed the cat, but since they've got nine lives (most of which are surrendered to the sound of screeching brakes and swearing drivers) they can afford a life of active, playful wondering. Children are much the same. *Don't touch that, it's hot. Don't touch that, it's hot. Don't touch that, it's – see, I told you, but you had to find out for yourself, didn't you?* Wild running – whether a literal or a figurative run into the dark – embraces curiosity. Makes 'finding out' fun. I'm reminded of Eleanor Roosevelt's great admonition: 'Do one thing every day that scares you'.

A 2010 report by the National Trust talked of how city dwellers are becoming 'terrified' of the countryside. Dame Fiona Reynolds, the Trust's Director General, said: 'It's urgent we reconnect people. We're breeding a society that's less confident about exploring, less confident about going to places we haven't been to before.'

People who are brought up in big cities are 'scared', and

see the countryside as 'a place full of unfamiliar and unexpected things. It's becoming this great unknown, alien place.'

Dame Fiona is right to be worried, but reversing this 'alienation' from the natural world means trying to see the bigger picture, a picture that includes oil spills, abandoned shopping trolleys and technology that dumbs us down rather than fires us up. Of course it's a good thing that we're now taught the value of recycling, but more important is learning the fundamental value (measured in muddy footsteps, in curiosity, in bravery) of our place on the earth and our natural obligation to look after it. And as runners, a good start would be to go out and have a good run on it, this earth we're trying to save.

44

When we were young we dreamt of adventure. Then as we got older we were taught that dreams of adventure are for the young, and we got scared by poverty, joblessness and the responsibilities of relationships and children. We grew up. For a while I was poor and jobless, unsure of anything other than wanting to sing, play a guitar, create. My 'problem' was my reluctance to give up dreaming those dreams of adventure; refusing to grow up. I clutched my copy of Frank Zappa's *Freak Out!* album, whose liner notes read: 'Drop out of school before your mind rots from our mediocre educational system.'

That was my mantra back then. I refused to believe that growing older meant giving up on being an explorer, a searcher. I threw myself into the world, into an adulthood full of home-made clothes and hitch-hiking, shared houses, protest marches, huge bonfire parties, a thousand part-time jobs, busking Undertones songs on Parisian streets, falling in and out and in and out of love. A whole series of adventures, none of them planned. Margaret Thatcher's decade came and went to my own soundtrack of four-part harmonies and football chants. I got married (her hair was green, mine was blue), arrested, laughed at and slagged off. Chumbawamba had a hit record, I turned forty playing Clash songs in the basement of a warehouse and, sometime between 9/11 and the invasion of Iraq, my daughter Maisy was born. And it was all an adventure; all of it. It still is.

Most good adventure stories, with their narrative arc of highs and lows, setbacks and survival, seem to end with the ghost of Edith Piaf singing as the red velvet curtains close in one grand, final swish. *Non, je ne regrette rien*. But it isn't true in my case. I have one regret: I didn't discover running until I was almost thirty years old. By running, I mean wild running, off-road running, mountain running. Adventure running. Since then my running – with its litany of purple bruises and spectacular views – has sewn itself like a thread through my life, a badly stitched, wonky, wiggly thread that is in places unpicked and worn and in places deceptively neat. Running has been a constant, albeit an unpredictable and continually surprising one. It works as a metaphor only in that it refuses regularity and repetition; it falls over, picks itself up, gets lost and sometimes, very occasionally, wins. There's very little pattern to it.

To runners with steady jobs that take up the bulk of the working week, I can only assume that such running would be all the more special, all the more extraordinary. Peculiar, exceptional and adventurous. Marathon racing can rarely be called an adventure – it can be meaningful and noteworthy but seldom peculiar. Too many traffic cones, too many watches.

One sports watch retailer begins its spiel by stating, 'Choosing the right model can be an arduous task for the fitness runner.' Arduous. What, arduous like the last three miles of the Pike's Peak ten-mile ascent, another 3,000 feet of uphill climbing? Arduous, like the long, rocky descent off Ingleborough? Or just arduous like choosing a watch? The 'fitness runner' will probably (apparently) have his or her eye on the latest overspeced GPS watch (in a dashing shade of blue). It records distance, pace, calories burnt and heart rate, as well as telling the time. 'Advanced training features will challenge you to step up your pace as you race against the watch's in-built training partner to improve your times.' (That's a real quote, by the way.) And a snip at just £220.

I regret not running during my youth if only for the simple fact of all that *missed adventure*. Running doesn't replace the rest of your life, it adds to it, balances against it, contributes to it. Widens the context of your work. Makes home look different. Gives an altered perspective to health, to the body's movement and breathing. All of this I see as an adventure, another chapter in the story.

> *Why do all the clerks and navvies in the railway trains look so sad and tired, so very sad and tired? I will tell you. It is because they know that their train is going right. It is because they know that whatever place they have a ticket for, that place they will reach. It is because after they have passed Sloane Square they know that the next station must be Victoria, and nothing but Victoria. Oh, their wild rapture! Oh, their eyes like stars and their souls again in Eden, if the next station were unaccountably Baker Street!* (G. K. Chesterton's, *The Man Who Was Thursday*)

The reason I didn't run for so long was because all I knew of running – other than watching the Olympic Games

– was the stiff, unyielding marathon. The twenty-week training plans, the dietary advice, the acres of TV-advertised super-white road-running shoes. I knew the pained expressions I saw on lunch-break runners' faces. The weary jogger's shuffle, the joyless treadmill. I have run, many times, on city streets. Trapped in hotels on month-long tours, determined and desperate to run, I've been up and down the backstreets, dual carriageways and market squares of scores of smog-choked cities, from Amsterdam to Rome, Istanbul to Chicago, Moscow to Aberdeen. These runs are often exploratory and frustrating; attempts to track down some grass. Discovering a walled park, a golf course or a canal bank can be disproportionately energizing and satisfying, justifying time otherwise spent rewriting lyrics, wandering around museums, churches or art galleries, or just watching BBC World News on the TV. But more often than not I've felt city road running to be a duty, something I ought to do rather than something I love to do. I heard it referred to recently as 'Chased by the Dog' running – running to escape the painful things in life like heart disease. In which case, it's functional and responsible; like sweeping the kitchen floor, say, or mowing the lawn. A twenty-six-mile-long, straight-line lawn.

Tokyo, 1989. We were playing a series of concerts there as part of a festival of international radical music, and we had a day off. Mount Fuji, on the outskirts of the city, was a bus ride away, its familiar iconic snow-peaked summit rising over 12,000 feet above the city's smog. Chumbawamba front man Dan and me were standing at the mountain's Kawaguchiko Fifth Station, from where we'd learnt that an ascent to the top of locally named Fuji-san was possible. We were wearing shorts and fell-running shoes, carrying limited food and essentials in bumbags, aware that most of the people we saw walking towards the summit were carrying small oxygen cylinders and walking sticks. The mountain is volcanic, and its surface terrain is coarse, black ash – like running on Yorkshire coalfield slag heaps. Undaunted, we set off running up one of the well-signposted paths, passing lines of tourists. The ancient Japanese believed Mount Fuji was the closest place to heaven that mortals could reach, and many made the long journey to the top to be within touching distance of the Shinto gods. As we ran, it became obvious that the mountain's rich history, coupled with the overphotographed view of the mountain from distance, belied Fuji's basic ugliness – especially during tourist season, when it vies for the crown of most walked mountain in the world (over 100,000 people climb Mount Fuji each year) and teems with people trekking slowly towards its volcanic rim.

It was actually (sad to say) a boring run to the summit, remarkable only for the amount of people wending their way up the zigzagging ascending path. There's a Japanese saying: 'A wise man climbs Mount Fuji once, a fool twice.' Now I knew why. The summit of the mountain was dirty and littered, its various mountaintop huts selling trinkets and canned drinks. It reminded me of a busy city-centre intersection, spattered with cheap advertising and hurried huddles of people. It was lamentable. It felt as if the mountain's dignity had been belittled by its sheer popularity. We spent a minute or two up there and then headed back down a different path, steeper and with fewer people. We did it; we climbed Fuji. It wasn't particularly difficult and it wasn't particularly inspiring, and whether it beats joining 35,000 other runners in the annual Tokyo Marathon, listening to Belinda Carlisle over the loudspeaker system as they set off, is debatable. I went looking for history and tradition, for something natural that transcended Tokyo's garish consumerism. I went looking for the peace and spirit of a mountain, for a natural connection to ancient civilizations, and all I got was this lousy T-shirt.

Interviewer: What are the relative merits of various human pursuits? For example, do you consider jogging to be of equal value to say creating art, on some cosmic scale?

Frank Zappa: No.

Interviewer: Why? What is the scale?

Frank Zappa: What is it that survives from ancient civilizations that characterizes that civilization? What do you find? Not jogging! Things that are related to art survive. The beautiful things that societies do is what survives.

45

French philosopher Michel de Montaigne, a brilliant and witty essayist and gallivanting sixteenth-century states-man, made his name by embracing the idea of doubt – celebrating the notion of not knowing, of mystery and puzzlement. We don't always have the answers, we don't always know the outcome. His honesty shocked polite society ('Kings and philosophers defecate, and so do ladies') just as his lack of spirituality and general championing of common sense made him unpopular among his contemporaries. Even during the Renaissance – that time of great cultural and philosophical change – Montaigne was considered a bit of a nutter. He deliberately left his most famous work *Essays* without a conclusion, asserting that the goal of the journey is unimportant; what is important is the journey itself. 'I undertake the journey neither to return from it nor to complete it; I undertake [it] only to move about while I like moving.'

Do you ever set off on a run, unsure of how long you'll be out? Do you ever consciously avoid making that decision? We're all so loaded down with the tick-tock time of deadlines and appointments that it's difficult to create space enough for that indecision, that mystery. When leaving the house, I'm often tempted to use Captain Oates' famous last words, 'I am just going outside and may be some time', uttered before he selflessly vanished into a blizzard on the ill-fated British Antarctic expedition of 1912. 'Some time': one of the pleasures of trail running is its incompatibility with accurately measured time, its forcible slowing down and speeding up. The gold clock traditionally awarded to retiring workers might as well have the word 'irony' ready engraved; *here's a constant reminder of a lifetime of subjugation to company time.*

There's a beautiful story taken from contemporary court witnesses at the time of the Luddite rebellion of 1812. The Luddites were a widespread army of working men, weavers, in the north of England, who had taken a secret oath to oppose the imposition of new weaving machinery in the mills. Theirs wasn't a fight against progress or technology, but against the terrible effects of that modernization – thousands of loyal and hard-working men faced unemployment, hunger and seeing their children condemned to the poorhouse as a result of the installation of the new cropping machines. The mill-owners had neither the obligation nor the willingness to help out the men and their families, content to throw men out of work and replace them with automated timber-and-steel cropping frames.

Neither was this a localized outbreak of lawlessness. The Luddites operated from most of the major northern towns and cities, gathering together after dark to halt the passage of the new frames across country to the mills. With the use of long-handled hammers, the machinery would be smashed to pieces and its transporters ordered to flee. The men had the support of the communities around them, safe in the knowledge that their identities could be kept secret; they acted not only out of self-preservation but in support of others across the various towns and counties of England. Petitions from the weavers and croppers demanding that the government intervene in the affair were met only with the defiant battle cry of laissez-faire:

> While the Committee fully acknowledge and most deeply lament the great distress of numbers of persons engaged in the cotton manufacture, they are of opinion that no interference of the legislature with the freedom of trade, or with the perfect liberty of every individual to dispose of his time and of his labour in the way and on the terms which he may judge most conducive to his own interest, can take place without violating general principles of the first importance to the prosperity and happiness of the community, without establishing the most pernicious precedent, or without aggravating, after a very short time, the pressure of the general distress, and imposing obstacles against that distress ever being removed. (Parliamentary Debates, 1812)

One of the mill-owners so bent on the use of the new machinery, with no regard for the men he was forcing into poverty, was William Cartwright, a pernicious and wealthy man who owned a mill at Rawfolds, near Halifax, Yorkshire. He not only introduced the new frames but spoke eloquently in their favour, encouraging other mill-owners to follow his lead. Expecting an attack, he employed a military guard of half a dozen armed men and fortified the mill, strengthening the doors, setting the stairwells with heavy spiked rollers to crush any attackers and keeping a large tank on the mill's roof holding several gallons of acid, ready to be poured on any Luddites. Sure enough, on a cold April evening in 1812, upwards of 300 Luddites gathered after dark from the towns and villages surrounding the mill, this self-styled 'army of redressers' gathering momentum as it marched haphazardly across field and moorland to reach Rawfolds.

The attack, which came in the dead of night and lasted for several hours, resulted in two of the Luddites being shot dead by Cartwright's militia and many others injured, including the sentries guarding the mill. Almost every window and door of the huge stone factory was smashed and broken; nevertheless, the hated cropping frames remained intact. Claiming victory, William Cartwright was determined to help the authorities hunt down and try the men who had been involved in the attack. Of the hundreds of Luddites who gathered that night, only a small number were ever brought to trial; what follows is the case of a man who, though accused, escaped the death penalty. Before we begin, let me once again quote Montaigne: *'Fear sometimes adds wings to the heels.'*

Some time before midnight during the attack on the mill at Rawfolds, a young Luddite named Rayner, either seeing or sensing the bloody debacle that the Luddites had walked into, decided to effect an escape. Rayner was from Brighouse, several miles away, and a close friend of one of the local Luddite leaders. He'd taken the oath of secrecy a few months earlier and now, fearing for his life should he be seen, he retraced his steps in the dark and, crouching low as he went, ran at full speed back towards his home village. Rayner was in fact the local champion cross-country runner, known for victories in foot races across the region, and his flight from the scene of the battle was to prove his greatest run of all. Despite the icy conditions and the gloom of the night he was able to race at high tempo across fields, along ditches and through plantations, following paths and trails he knew well and cutting corners to avoid the roadways.

He arrived back in Brighouse just twenty minutes after leaving Rawfolds – a remarkable time – and as he entered the village he made for the chapel that stood in its centre, darting between houses and up winding alleyways until he stood at the front gate of the church. The church warden appeared, bemused and interested to see Rayner up at this hour – it was by now barely minutes before midnight and the warden was doing his rounds, locking up the heavy doors of the church. Rayner and the warden exchanged pleasantries for a while, Rayner relaxed and calm. The clock struck, and, as it did so, both men joined in a count of the church bells. To their amusement, it struck thirteen times. Laughing at the peculiarity, the warden explained that the clock had been repaired that afternoon and was obviously still in need of some work. At this, Rayner sauntered home and retired to bed.

Over the next few weeks, through the work of several hired detectives from London, magistrates were pleased to have a number of suspected Luddites brought before the courts. One such was Rayner, handed over to the detectives by an informer named Carter and now facing the assizes, accused not only of being a member of the Luddites but of participating in the attack at Rawfolds. The magistrate was a Mr Ratcliffe of Huddersfield, a man firmly on the side of the manufacturers, grimly determined to send as many of the rebels as possible to York Castle to be hanged. Ratcliffe first cross-examined the informant, Carter, who explained exactly when Rayner had last been seen at the site of the attack. Twenty minutes before midnight, he stated. Then the church warden was called; he testified of the memorable encounter he'd had with Rayner in Brighouse that night, notable for the clock having struck thirteen as they talked. Several other witnesses from the village testified to the accuracy of this peculiar event. The magistrate re-examined both Carter and the warden, stressing the importance of their testimony regarding the timing of Rayner's flight and arrival. Assessing the distance from Rawfolds to Brighouse across country as four miles, the annoyed and frustrated Mr Ratcliffe was left with little option but to set Rayner at liberty, as, unaware of Rayner's reputation as a cross-country runner, he was unable to accept that any man could cover such a distance across rough ground in so short a time. *'The clock talked loud. I threw it away, it scared me what it talked.'* (Tillie Olsen, American writer and social activist)

46

As I write this book, it changes. It changes as I try to respond to the swirling, windblown ideas and arguments that crowd out the first fifteen minutes of every day's run; before I've relaxed into a rhythmic, attentive stride, before I've stopped to look at a huge frog with colouring exactly matching that of the rotting leaves around it. This book is written as I run, and its unexpected changes in direction are there because, following my feet, that's where my head takes me.

'Running is a metaphor for life' apparently. So far while writing the book I've avoided this cliché like I'd avoid a mid-summer road race in Florida. But I think it may be time to crack the egg and have a quick dip in its runny contents – yes, running is a metaphor for life. It's the easy equation that gets used, used, and used again in those rows of yes-I-did-it books on running that I found in that huge redbrick Barnes & Noble bookstore all those months ago. The popularity of this ease-of-use metaphor seems to come from a quasi-spiritual view that our lives are journeys; that there's a start line, a hard bit in the middle and a finish line. And there the usefulness of 'running is a metaphor for life' ends, since the most popular form of running – in straight lines, along city streets – actually bears little resemblance to life.

Life twists and turns. It goes up and down. It weaves through, climbs above, bends around, ducks under. Doesn't it? Thus, I propose an amendment to the sport's most well-worn cliché, and this is it: 'Running is a metaphor for life, as long as you leave the harsh imposition of the grid system and head off along twisting, turning forest tracks, follow plunging valleys, ford streams, scale hills and get lost and mucky on the way.'

If your life is, in fact, conducted in straight lines, with very little meandering or stopping to marvel at things, if your life is circumscribed, fenced-in, girdled, restricted, walled and railed – well, it isn't just time to change your running habits, it's time to change your life. There's a film called *Spirit of the Marathon* which eulogizes (quite beautifully) the Chicago Marathon with broad sweeps of nonsensical Positive Thinking and slow-motion shots of grimacing athletes (always a winning combination). In it, former marathon champion Dick Beardsley, now a professional motivational speaker, asserts 'when you cross that finish line, no matter how slow, or how fast – it will change your life forever'. Sadly, Dick is wrong. The Chicago Marathon is a 26.2-mile race around a city centre, when all's said and done, and, though it counts as a huge achievement for many people, it hardly qualifies as 'life-changing'. Having children is life-changing, poverty, war and imprisonment are life-changing, the death and serious illness of loved ones is life-changing – not a few hours running around a city centre.

Runner and writer Mark Will-Weber unashamedly tells a story of how, on his honeymoon night in Lucerne, he and his new bride arrived at their hotel during a rainstorm.

At which point, he writes, '. . . *and I had not yet run*'. After quickly changing, he stands in the hotel lobby for ten minutes waiting for the rain to abate. It does not (oh! how the world can get in the way of a run). Finally, after much prevarication, he makes a dash for it, heading for a locally famous covered bridge. 'I was drenched before I got there,' he writes, before admitting to spending fifteen or twenty minutes trotting back and forth under the covered bridge, with the rain 'thundering on the roof – my shoes making a squishy sound with each step, like someone was squeezing a sponge'. After what Will-Weber deems a suitable interval, and with 'a pretence of dignity and dedication', he sprints back to the hotel.

Now this is puzzling on so many counts (not least of which is the author's fear of running in the rain). Running needs perspective and context, it needs to be balanced – the context being the rest of your life. That big, beautiful, messy stuff, with its humdrum and chaos and (seemingly) with its honeymoon hotels full of newly-wed brides pacing their rooms waiting for the completion of your daily ten kilometres. In the course of writing this book, I applied to the New York City Marathon race committee for a media pass – an official badge that might make it possible for me to speak to runners and volunteers before and after the race. Having no official position as a journalist I wrote to the editor of the English Fell Runners' Association magazine, Britta Sendlhofer, asking her to act as quasi-official back-up. I explained to her that I was writing '. . . a book that might put forward an eloquent case for leaving the roads behind and rediscovering the world that isn't paved, layered in tarmac and surrounded by huge buildings and pollution. Of course, I haven't told the NYC marathon organisers this!'

She replied saying of course she'd support my application (I'd had various articles published in *The Fellrunner* magazine), before adding, 'I did NY once in 2002 and actually really enjoyed it :)', which, while not making me feel guilty, did prompt the conundrum of how to so scathingly dismiss city-centre marathon racing while not belittling or ignoring the obvious fulfilment experienced by so many city marathon runners. Because it's not that I resent so much the three, four or five hours spent on the tarmac on that one day, but the monstrous, overboiled mythology that accompanies it; a mythology so weighty and dominant that it blinds people to other possibilities.

What wild running offers, without tending to filmic, close-up hyperbole, is not something life-*changing* but a chance to experience something life-*affirming*. A running that knits into life, explores life and demonstrates life. That practically throws life in your face at every step. Every step – for the problem with that tired clichéd metaphor is that it presupposes (as well as a start and a middle) an end, a finish line, a death. Dick Beardsley's words aren't about the race, they're about the finish. To hell with the rest of it, the monotony and the pain and the feeling-like-you're-about-to-vomit, all that matters is the finish line. (In life, of course, the finish line is the bit we all want to avoid.)

Ursula Le Guin said, 'it is good to have an end to journey toward; but it is the journey that matters, in the end'. Of all the many hundreds of races I've run, I remember very few finish lines. I remember views and people, rockfalls and scrambles, getting lost, wild animals, lashing

269

storms. There are some finish lines I remember, if I try hard enough: I remember finishing a leg of the Calderdale Way Relay in the mid-1990s because I crossed the line with my injured running partner on my shoulders. I remember finishing along the village street in the Burnsall race, mainly because everyone was urging the runner behind to catch me. I certainly don't remember finishing the 1981 Bolton Marathon – and no, it didn't change my life.

So let me try again: 'Off-road running is a metaphor for life – on the assumption that we don't know exactly where we're going, we may get lost, we'll probably have to stop somewhere to take stock of the magnificent surroundings, we may spend huge amounts of time clambering over, under or through things, and by the time we're almost finished we'll be too busy marvelling at what we've just experienced to notice we got to the end.'

That'll do. I want a life like that.

And no, I didn't get an official press pass for the New York City Marathon; quite simply, they never replied.

47

Sunday evening, and the last runner crosses the finishing line in New York's Central Park almost ten hours after the race began, walking through the flotsam and jetsam of a long day's madness – wraparound body-insulation blankets, photographers, officials, cups, banners, a jam-packed theatre of ads, T-shirts, slogans and brightly coloured plastic. It's dark now, but there's still a spontaneous swell of applause. Of the 45,300 starters, 44,829 have finished. That's less than 500 dropouts – clearly this is a race that's designed, from start to finish, to pump the maximum number of bodies around its arteries. For hours now they've been spilling into this fenced-off, funnelled finish, stumbling and collapsing, some barely able to stand upright.

The Chilean miner, Edison Peña, with both knees having been wrapped in ice for much of the race, staggered across the line in just under six hours, grimacing with pain and exhaustion. Race officials rushed to him as he stumbled towards a safety barrier, congratulating him – he couldn't raise a smile. Race favourite Haile Gebrselassie, on what the TV commentators described (without irony) as 'the steep, unforgiving descent coming over the Queensboro Bridge', dropped out suffering from an existing knee injury, informing reporters straight afterwards of his retirement from running.

Central Park begins to switch off, a pool of darkness in the illuminated city, apart from the area around the marathon finish – a tangle of arc-lit marquees and vehicles, officials with clipboards criss-crossing between a line of UPS vans dispensing the last of the personal bags brought over from Staten Island. The surviving scoopfuls of bewildered runners are helped to their feet and guided out onto Manhattan's roads, where police fight against the natural flow of bodies, shouting and waving and trying to keep the Sunday evening traffic moving. It all looks utterly strange.

Those 44,829 runners can tick that box that says they worked towards something, put the effort in, and made it happen. It's commendable – the whole day is a slowly sung hymn to sacrifice and dedication, to triumph and relief. I don't want to end this book sounding mean-spirited. I applaud these people who've put so much effort into the day. If it spurs them on to run more, to feel better about themselves and what they're capable of, then it's been worth it.

Perhaps, though, there'll come a time when people get tired of these concrete jamborees. When we'll get bored of being funnelled and directed, herded and sectioned. We'll decide that the city, marvellous as it may be, isn't a place for running marathons. And we'll look away from the skyscrapers and the traffic jams, the stop signs and the go lights and the clutter of street furniture battling for attention. We'll look beyond the city centres and the suburban detached housing and the projects and the malls and we'll see that, some-where over there, the pavement runs out and gives way to grass and trees and fields. And we'll see that there are paths and tracks and trails crossing the land, as far as the legs can run and further than the eye can see. And once we take tentative steps onto those trails – well, we might never go back to plod-plod-plodding along First Avenue.

48

I did, in fact, run a marathon this year. Really – the sacred 26.2 miles. There were no cheering crowds, no Gatorade drinks stations and no blue line to follow. Just a bright, fresh day in early summer – at the end of this year mapped out in trails and seasons – and both sides of the sprawling, rampant Brandywine Valley to explore. Together with Casey I wanted to see what it was like to run the distance, on my own terms – no roads, no traffic, no plastic cones – just a vague route, a borrowed GPS watch and a day to fill (a day to fill is a rare privilege that has to be snatched, squeezed and hugged to death). What can I say? It was a day of trees, rivers, hawks, bloody legs, open fields, birdsong, cheese sandwiches and trail mix. A day to remember, without a commemorative T-shirt or photo to remember it by. And, really, I ran it for this book. I thought it might be an interesting thing to do. In the end, it got me a good day out and a paragraph, and that was enough. If I look back over the year I've spent in America, it's a year of good days out. The running and the races are a diary, often gloriously jumbled, a year of rainstorms, leaf piles, mud, snow, swollen rivers, granite and brush and grass. A year of planting my feet on the changing earth.

So the year, this book and the cycle of seasons come to

an end. Well, not really. Spring turns into summer and the familiarity of lush greens and long days returns. When this book finishes, when I'm done with this particular year's adventure and when you've closed the last page and put the book up there on the shelf between all the marathon training manuals (I'm kidding), the seasons will continue, rolling on, bigger and more resilient than any of us. And of course we carry on running, running through the revolving, evolving world, seeing its forests and mountains and rivers change with the seasons.

Despite my continuing horror at the life-sucking version of running that is the city marathon, I knew I couldn't end with that vision of the plod-plod-plod along First Avenue. I wanted to finish with a run I did sometime in February, in a small town called Twisp in Washington state. A few miles out of town, staying with friends along a deep-sided valley, baby Johnny – then seven months old and crawling – had settled into a pattern of waking before the sun, eager to worm his way out of bed and across the floor, dying to make new discoveries. My days had changed – being awake and dressed at 5 a.m. didn't seem strange any more. On one such morning I threw on running clothes and headed out and up the valley side into the dense dark of pre-dawn, up a pathless, scrubby and steep silhouette of a hill towards a summit outlined by the paling moonlight.

And as the sky ever so slowly turned from black to darkest blue, a faint glow appeared on the far horizon, before creeping tentatively across the landscape with a wash of orange. I was reminded of how I began this book, with a run in the Lake District in England, two shadows cast by moon and sun as I stood on a mountaintop. Here in Twisp, almost 5,000 miles away, I carried on running, racing the sun to the top of the hill. I got there and stood to watch the sun break fully and spectacularly over the low mountains to the east, saw the moon hanging there directly opposite, watched my two shadows on the ground. The valley filled with light and I took a breath before setting off, smiling at my fortune, and at the world, and at this wonderful thing I'm able to do – run wild.

With Thanks

Casey, Maisy, Johnny

Christian Brett, Mark Hodkinson & Eliza Amon
For telling me that this was the book I ought to write,
before I started writing it.

David Luxton
For making sure this book didn't sit forlornly (and forever)
on my computer's hard drive.

Rhea Halford
For editing, ruthlessly and sympathetically.

Jay Griffiths & Richard Askwith
For being supportive to the point of cheerleading. How
uplifting, from two of my favourite writers.

Corinne Silva
For reading the early draft and putting me in touch with:
Kester Aspden
For reading that same draft and urging me to approach
the agent of:

Anthony Clavane
Who supported my decision to send the book to David Luxton, who milked the cow with the crumpled horn that tossed the dog that worried the cat that killed the rat that ate the malt that lay in the house that Jack built.

Adam Korn
Who believed in this book when his publishers didn't.
Bridget Wagner
Who suggested great changes.

… and the runners who commented, inspired, tagged along, ran in front:

Jim Whalley (of course)
Sarah Rowell
Geoff Read
Graham Schofield
Ray Hearne
Brian Stevenson
Jonathan Parsons
Charlie Macintosh
Gary Devine
Danbert Nobacon

Text Acknowledgments

Campos, Joseph J.; 'Travel Broadens The Mind', *Infancy Volume* 1(issue 2), pp149–219, 2000.

Dalton, Gilbert; 'The Tough of the Track' from The Rover #1331, December 30th 1950

Kimm, Dr Sue YS MD; Glynn, Nancy W PhD; Obarzanek, Eva PhD; Kriska, Andrea M PhD; Daniels, Stephen R MD; Barton, Bruce A PhD; Liu, Kiang PhD; 'Relation between the changes in physical activity and body-mass index during adolescence: a multicentre longitudinal study' Reported in The Lancet, 23 July 2005

Murakami, Haruki; *What I Talk About When I Talk About Running*, (Harvill Secker; Reprint edition 2008)

Whalley, Boff; Watts, Louise; Ferguson, Neil and Abbott, Judith; 'You Can' Words and Music © 2005, Reproduced by Permission of EMI Music Publishing Ltd, London W8 5SW

Winterson, Jeannette, *Written on the Body* (Vintage New Ed edition, 2010)